BEING HUMAN

HUMAN-COMPUTER INTERACTION IN THE YEAR 2020

Edited by Richard Harper, Tom Rodden, Yvonne Rogers and Abigail Sellen

Being Human: Human-Computer Interaction in the year 2020

Editors: Richard Harper, Tom Rodden, Yvonne Rogers and Abigail Sellen

ISBN: 978-0-9554761-1-2

Publisher: Microsoft Research Ltd

7 J J Thomson Avenue, Cambridge, CB3 0FB, England

The question persists and indeed grows whether the computer will make it easier or harder for human beings to know who they really are, to identify their real problems, to respond more fully to beauty, to place adequate value on life, and to make their world safer than it now is.

Norman Cousins – The Poet and the Computer, *1966*

Contents

About this Report

In March 2007, Microsoft Research organised the 'HCI 2020' meeting at the El Bulli Hacienda Hotel near Seville, Spain. The event's title expressed its key question: what will Human-Computer Interaction (HCI) be like in the year 2020? That question is important because HCI, significant as it was in the late 20th century, has a pivotal part to play in the 21st, when computers will become so pervasive that how humans interact with them will be a crucial issue for society.

HCI 2020 produced many ideas, both thrilling and troubling. This report is not a conventional publication of an academic conference but seeks to convey the passion of those ideas, both for the general reader and the HCI practitioner. For the general reader, this is important because knowledge of what the future might be may empower, while ignorance harm. For the HCI practitioner, its purpose is to map out the terrain and suggest new approaches while keeping an eye on the main prize: the embodiment of human values at the heart of computing.

This two-day forum brought together academics from the fields of computing, design, management science, sociology and psychology to debate, contribute to, and help formulate the agenda for Human-Computer Interaction in the next decade and beyond. Participants also came from the commercial world, including representatives from software companies, hardware manufacturers, and content providers.

The forum was convened because the field of HCI has moved on and matured in many significant ways since its emergence in the early 1980s. Over the years, a number of influential books and articles have helped to shape its goals and perspectives. As HCI has developed, many of the questions posed by its past research agendas have been answered, while others have become less important with the passing of time. Computing itself has moved on from what was possible when HCI first developed. As a result, many members of the HCI community have begun to voice concerns that HCI needs a new agenda if it is to continue to be relevant for the 21st century.

If there was one thing that the participants in this forum had in common, it was a recognition that any new direction for HCI would need to place human values at its core. The great accomplishment of HCI has been, to date, that it allows investigations of matters beyond what one might call the mechanics of the interface, such things as the design of the graphical user interface, and of keyboards and of mice. Its success now allows researchers to focus on how computers can support human-to-human concerns, rather than simply human-machine interaction. HCI has helped to produce a world in which interacting with computers is easier and richer. The real HCI issues now include what might be our aspirations, our desires for self-understanding and expression, and our willingness to use imagination to create a different future.

The questions that result are far-reaching and profound. HCI can no longer be solely the scientific investigation of *what* role technology might have – it will need to be part of the empirical, philosophical and moral investigation of *why* technology has a role. It will entail asking new questions about how we ought to interact with technology in this new world and it will even entail asking what the use of computing implies about our conceptions of society. Even philosophical questions will be important. For example, our concepts of how the mind works will affect the way we design technologies to support memory, intelligence and much more besides. All of this implies that other disciplines from the Arts and Humanities will become more relevant as the remit of HCI becomes broader.

The goal of the forum was therefore to uncover and articulate new paradigms, goals and perspectives for HCI.

By bringing together some of the world's leading thinkers on this topic, the hope was that their discussions, debates and scholarly commentaries would help define how HCI can deliver this 'human face' of computing.

This report is the result of that forum. It is not a record of the papers presented or discussions held, but a distillation, an attempt to capture the spirit of what concerned and excited the participants, looking ahead to 2020. It describes how the world around us has changed and continues to change, and how the design of computers is helping to create a new socio-digital landscape. It explains how the field of HCI can contribute to making this landscape one that reflects the values we hold as well as provide opportunities for the expression of diversity in those values. Being human is not simply a label; it is about a set of aspirations. Recognising those aspirations and striving to realise them can make the world we live in one to celebrate rather than fear.

Needless to say, this report cannot encompass all the issues that this ambition implies, just as it cannot relay all the topics raised by the participants at the forum. While we have endeavoured to represent, as much as possible, the views of the contributors, its main purpose is to entice the reader, whoever that might be, to think more seriously about the role of computing in our everyday lives. If it can further highlight the importance of a new kind of HCI in making 2020 the kind of future we want it to be, so much the better.

Last but not least, we would like to thank: all the participants in HCI 2020, and the organisations and institutions that supported them; Sarah Cater who organised the event; Vicki Ward and Rachel Howard for public relations and marketing; Angela Still for local support; Denise Stanley who facilitated the event;

Stephen Emmott for advice and guidance; Bill Buxton who inspired the title of this report; book designer Nick Duffield; designer Richard Banks for helping with images; editor Peter Bradley; and our careful printer, Piggott Black Bear. Finally, a special thanks to the director of Microsoft Research Cambridge, Andrew Herbert, who gave the green light for this event and made it possible.

Richard Harper
Professor of Socio-Digital Systems and Senior Researcher, Microsoft Research Cambridge, UK

Tom Rodden
Professor of Computing, Nottingham University, UK

Yvonne Rogers
Professor in Human-Computer Interaction, Open University, UK

Abigail Sellen
Senior Researcher, Microsoft Research Cambridge, UK

Conveners of the HCI 2020 Forum, 2007

Contacting Us

We welcome feedback on this report. All comments should be addressed to:

Richard Harper or Abigail Sellen
Microsoft Research
7 J J Thomson Avenue
Cambridge, CB3 0FB, UK

r.harper@microsoft.com
asellen@microsoft.com

General Introduction

The world we live in has become suffused with computer technologies. They have created change and continue to create change. It is not only on our desktops and in our hands that this is manifest; it is in virtually all aspects of our lives, in our communities, and in the wider society of which we are a part.

What will our world be like in 2020? Digital technologies will continue to proliferate, enabling ever more ways of changing how we live. But will such developments improve the quality of life, empower us, and make us feel safer, happier and more connected? Or will living with technology make it more tiresome, frustrating, angst-ridden, and security-driven? What will it mean to be human when everything we do is supported or augmented by technology? What role can researchers, designers and computer scientists have in helping to shape the future?

The aim of this report is to reflect upon the changes afoot and outline a new paradigm for understanding our relationship with technology. A more extensive set of lenses, tools and methods is needed that puts human values centre stage. And here, both positive and negative aspects need to be considered: on the one hand, people use technology to pursue healthier and more enjoyable lifestyles, expand their creative skills with digital tools, and instantly gain access to information never before available. On the other, governments become more reliant on computers to control society, criminals become more cunning via digital means, and people worry more about what information is stored about them.

The report is divided into four parts. In Part 1, we look back over the past 20 years or so, charting some of the major changes in computing, living and society and suggest where we are going. In Part 2, we outline how these changes are transforming the nature of our interaction with computers, and specify key questions that need to be addressed in the next 15 years as a result. Part 3 is concerned with Human-Computer Interaction (HCI) as a field of research and as a community of practitioners and designers. This part proposes an agenda for how the field can move forward by focusing on human values. Part 4, Recommendations, outlines specific suggestions for HCI in terms of how the field needs to change. For those who are new to the field of HCI, there is an Appendix giving an overview of the field, a brief sense of its history, and a description of some of its main achievements.

1 Our Changing World

Major changes have occurred within the computer revolution; changes which encompass all aspects of its role. These are not just quantitative in nature, such as exponential increases in processing power and storage capacity, but are more fundamental, pointing not only to the function of computer technology, but its emerging diversity both in terms of its form and place in the world. Computers are now embedded within a huge range of materials and artefacts, and take on roles in almost all aspects of life. People and lifestyles are altering. These changes are sometimes spurred on by technology, but other times work in parallel or provoke technological innovation. There is a global scale of change which is taking place hand in hand with new technologies. This gives rise to tensions between individuals and governments, and between globalisation and cultural diversity. In this Part, we comment on change at all levels, and provide pointers to where we are going in future.

The world of the future: utopia ➔
or dystopia? It is within our
power to decide.

13

1.1 Changing Computers

There have been various computer-driven revolutions in the past: the widespread introduction of the personal computer (PC) was one, the invention of the graphical browser was another, and the Internet yet another. There have also been computer eras where one type of computer has dominated, having straightforward implications for whether the computers were shared or personal, and for whether they were specialised commodities or not *(see diagram below)*. But the ways computers have altered our lives, all aspects of our lives, is more comprehensive than, at first blush, recollections of these technological revolutions or eras might suggest.

Computers affect how we undertake the most prosaic of activities – from buying food to paying our bills – and they do so in ways we might not have imagined when the first personal computers arrived on our desks. They have also created wholly new experiences, for example, allowing us to inhabit virtual worlds with people from many different parts of the globe. In between these extremes, from the prosaic to the wholly new, computers have taken over from older technologies in ways that looked merely like substitution at first but which have ended up creating radical change.

Four Computing Eras ➔

1

1960s: Mainframe Era
One computer per many users.

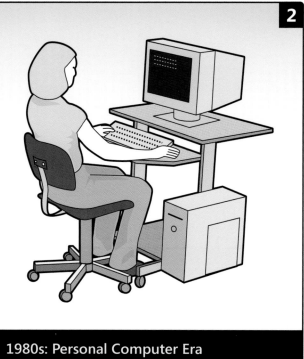

2

1980s: Personal Computer Era
One computer per user.

Photography, for example, has retained its familiarity despite moving from being chemically-based to being digital. At the point of creation, people still 'point and shoot' in much the same way as they used to.

However, what one can do with images when they are digital is quite different. Whereas, before, we may have only printed one or two rolls of film, displaying the photos on the mantelpiece or in an album, digital images are now reproduced many times over, and are often broadcast around the world on websites. The activities we undertake and the goals we have in mind

when we take photos and share them, then, are not at all the same now as they were even five years ago.

It is not just in terms of user experiences, such as shopping, games, and picture-taking that the world has changed. Computers have altered our sense of the world at large, letting us see images of far-away places, instantaneously and ubiquitously. The world, now, seems so much smaller than it was even a decade ago. In this section we begin to look at many different aspects of how computing technologies have changed and their impact on our lives.

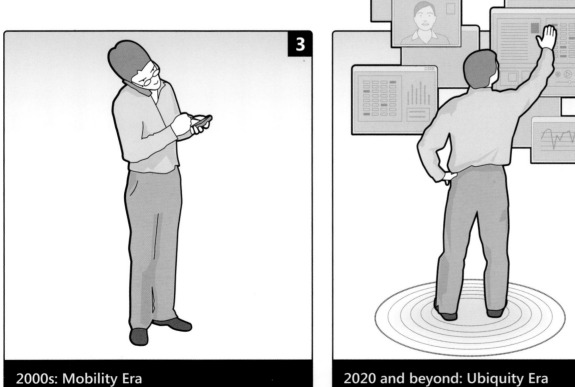

3

2000s: Mobility Era
Several computers per user.

4

2020 and beyond: Ubiquity Era
Thousands of computers per user.

GUIs to Gestures

Most of us learned how to use a computer by interacting with a personal computer, using a keyboard and mouse to point, click and select icons and options from menus. We began with creating documents by using word processors, doing calculations using spreadsheets and making fancy slide shows using presentation applications. Input to the computer was fairly intuitive, drawing on the metaphor of a virtual desktop, that allowed us to do all these tasks through the 'graphical user interface' or GUI *(for this and other terms used throughout, see the Glossary)*, allowing us to interact with graphical objects on the screen rather than relying solely on typed commands.

The GUI has dominated the way we interact with computers for over twenty years. In many ways it is quite forgiving: typos slip into every sentence but we do not worry because we have automatic spell checkers, changing our 'hte's to 'the's without us even noticing. Likewise, we frequently select the wrong window or menu option but know we can quickly 'undo' such slips of the fingers. But in other ways it is less than perfect. Many of us suffer from backache and some of us RSI as we relentlessly pound the keys and squeeze the mouse for hours on end. Remarkably, most of us put up with these problems. Researchers have known for years that pointing, clicking and dragging are not ideal forms of interaction for many tasks. Try drawing a flower or signing your name using a mouse.

The Reactable: a multi-touch interface for playing music. Performers can simultaneously interact with it by moving and rotating physical objects on its surface. Reactable was developed by Sergi Jordà and colleagues at the Universitat Pompeu Fabra, Barcelona. Icelandic songstress Björk used one on her 2007 tour. ➔

In the last few years, new input techniques have been developed that are richer and less prone to the many shortcomings of keyboard and mouse interaction. For example, there are tablet computers that use stylus-based interaction on a screen, and even paper-based systems that digitally capture markings made on specialised paper using a camera embedded in a pen. These developments support interaction through sketching and handwriting. Speech-recognition systems too support a different kind of 'natural' interaction, allowing people to issue commands and dictate through voice. Meanwhile, multi-touch surfaces enable interaction with the hands and the fingertips on touch-sensitive surfaces, allowing us to manipulate objects digitally as if they were physical.

From GUIs to multi-touch, speech to gesturing, the ways we interact with computers are diversifying as never before. Two-handed and multi-fingered input is providing a more natural and flexible means of interaction beyond the single point of contact offered by either the mouse or stylus. The shift to multiple points of input also supports novel forms of interaction where people can share a single interface by gathering around it and interacting together *(see the 'Reactable', left)*.

Tangible interfaces have also been developed, where everyday physical objects are embedded with computation, being able to sense and react to the ways they are picked up, manipulated, and moved in space. This approach has already found its way into a broad range of toys and game systems such as the Nintendo Wii. Camera and pressure input has also been developed that enables the movement of our whole body to control the computer, such as pressure pads in Dance Revolution and the use of video tracking in Sony's Eye Toy games.

The ability to sense our interaction without direct physical engagement with computer systems or input devices is also

a growing trend. Eye movements have been used for many years as a way of supporting the disabled in interacting with computers, but now we are also seeing the advent of 'brain-computer interfaces'. Such systems allow, for example, people with severe physical disabilities to use their brain waves to interact with their environment. Real-time brainwave activity is beginning to be used to control digital movies, turn on music, and switch the lights on and off. These interfaces can even control robot arms, allowing paralysed individuals to manipulate objects.

Input can also be a by-product of our activities in the world at large. For example, our location can be sensed through GPS and our movements can be captured using CCTV cameras, providing inputs to a range of interactive technologies. Low-cost Radio Frequency Identification (RFID) tags can also be tracked and provide new forms of information that can be fed into supply chains. These examples reflect how by 2020, embedded forms of computing will be increasingly commonplace, determining what actions to take based on where we are, how we move and what we are doing.

↑ The HotHand device: a ring worn by electric guitar players that uses motion sensors and a wireless transmitter to create different kinds of sound effects by various hand gestures.

17

VDUs to Smart Fabrics

The fixed video display units (VDUs) of the 1980s are being superseded by a whole host of flexible display technologies and 'smart' fabrics. Displays are being built in all sizes, from the tiny to the gigantic, and soon will become part of the fabric of our clothes and our buildings. By 2020, these advances are likely to have revolutionised the form that computers will take. For example, organic matter is being experimented with to create electronic components such as light emitting diodes. Recent advances in Organic Light Emitting Diodes (OLEDs) and plastic electronics are enabling displays to be made much more cheaply, with higher resolution and lower power consumption, some without requiring a backlight to function. OLEDs are an emissive electroluminescent layer made from a film of organic compounds, enabling a matrix of pixels to emit light of different colours. Plastic electronics also use organic materials to create very thin semi-conductive transistors that can be embedded in all sorts of materials, from paper to cloth,

enabling, for example, the paper in books or newspapers to be digitised. Electronic components and devices, such as Micro-Electro-Mechanical Systems (MEMS), are also being made at an extremely small size, allowing for very small displays.

New displays can be as much about 'input' as they are about 'output'. For example, they can be reactive to touch, can detect whole body movements and can be programmed to sense aspects of crowd behaviour and the environment. The diversity of interaction types now possible through displays will significantly affect how content is shown, how often and by whom. In particular, the ways advertising, public information, sports, concerts and other cultural events are presented and interacted with will take on innovative forms. We will have a video copy on our mobile phone of the goal we just saw on the pitch in front of us, for example. Likewise, how we read, whom we read with and when we read will change considerably when paper is re-imageable, and when screens can be folded, rolled up and even stretched.

Animated Textiles developed by Studio subTela at the Hexagram Institute, Montreal, Canada. These two jackets 'synch up' when the wearers hold hands, and the message scrolls from the back of one person to the other. ➔

Clothing manufacturers have started experimenting with how to embed computer systems using BlueTooth technology. High-end running shoes have sensors in them that talk to portable music players and other mobile devices providing information about how far the wearer has run, and at what speed, helping to update a training log. RFID tags are also becoming miniaturised and ever cheaper. Medical monitoring devices that can be worn on the body are also beginning to appear that provide dynamic readouts, reporting and alerting us to the status of various bodily functions (eg glucose level, cholesterol level). As newer technologies emerge that allow biological materials (nerves and tissues) to link with silicon circuitry, our relationship with computers will become even more intimate. Silicon and biological material will be knitted in new ways, enabling new forms of direct inputs and outputs implantable in our bodies. This shift will have profound effects on where we might see computers and what our relationship will be with them.

Handsets to the World in our Hands

A widespread and dramatic development in the everyday use of computers is the global explosion of mobile devices. From virtually nothing twenty or twenty-five years ago, mobile phones are rapidly becoming the most ubiquitous form of computing. From Shanghai to Swansea, Budikote to Birmingham, almost a third of the world's population carries a mobile phone. Add this staggering number to the music players and cameras pushed in people's pockets and it's not hard to see that a very significant part of the digital future will fit into the palm of our hands.

Many of the current generation of mobile devices, however, provide a frustrating 'genie-in-a-bottle' experience – they have incredible power trapped in a constraining case with a small screen and tricky-to-use input devices. Clever software visualisation techniques – such as automatic zooming – have helped to expand the interface. More recently, Apple's iPhone has shown how a multi-touch surface can turn mobile interaction into a much more pleasurable experience. Sensors of many types – from GPS location receivers and accelerometers to RFID tag scanners – and some actuators – like vibrotactile displays – are also being embedded into mobile devices to allow new forms of interaction. For example, the iPhone's various sensors detect when a person is putting their device next to their face, automatically switching it into a listening and speaking mode.

Of course, mobile devices are capable of much more than communication. Many such devices aim to deliver the desktop experience in the hand. We can now access our files, surf the Web and run many of the same applications as on our PCs. More than this, the world of mobile phones is now merging with mobile music and video players. Increasingly, they also let us monitor the world around us. Through BlueTooth and WiFi networks, we can see who else is in the area, discover what

Talk to the hand... From the first mobile phone 'brick' to the latest Apple iPhone: as the size reduces, the potential expands.

wireless connections are in the surrounding ether, and reveal a host of otherwise invisible services and applications. Some devices can also monitor our medical condition, too, such as blood pressure and heart rate. Mobile devices offer up a new window on the world, and provide us with a growing collection of tools for our working lives, social lives, and personal entertainment.

Many new forms of mobile interaction are on the horizon. Mobile devices will allow us to connect with others in new ways, as well as to access information in the environment. For example, we will increasingly be able to use mobile devices to interact with objects in the real world, acting more as if they are extensions of our own hands, by pointing and gesturing with them. While travelling, we can gesture with our mobile device at a historic building and be offered up an audio or visual history of its architecture. Taking a picture of a product in the supermarket can send us back information about where the product came from, its associated air miles, and ecological credentials. Likewise, buying a piece of music by pointing at a band's poster and then sending it as a gift to a friend's music player can be as natural as a 'cut and paste' operation on a desktop computer. As we move toward 2020, mobile devices will increasingly offer flexibility in interaction and new kinds of connections to both our local and remote world.

Simple Robots to Autonomous Machines That Learn

Emotional kitty: a robot hardware platform called iCAT uses a set of logical rules to convey emotional states as it makes decisions, with the goal of improving human-robot interaction. It looks confused if it's in trouble, smiles if it gets something right... ↓

Robots have been with for us for some time, most notably as characters in science fiction movies, but also as part of assembly lines, as remote investigators of hazardous situations (eg nuclear power stations, bomb disposal sites), and as search and rescue helpers in disasters (eg fires) or far away places (eg Mars). More recently, domestic robots have begun appearing in our homes as autonomous helpers. For example, robots are being developed to help the elderly and disabled with certain activities, such as picking up objects and cooking meals. The Roomba vacuum cleaner has also become a commercial success; it can be left alone to automatically navigate its way around owners' homes cleaning as it goes. The BEAR ('battlefield extraction and retrieval') is another kind of robot developed by the military, designed to find, pick up and rescue people in harm's way. Pet robots, in the guise of human companions, are also being commercialised, having first become a big hit in Japan. The robots provide a companion to talk to or cuddle, as if they were pets or dolls. The appeal of these kinds of robots is thought to be partially due to their therapeutic qualities, being able to reduce stress and loneliness among the elderly and infirm.

While the vision of widespread co-habitation with robots is beyond the 2020 horizon, recent advances in machine-learning techniques are being experimented with to model and support human behaviour in other ways. Knowing what a person is thinking or wanting will enable robots to be programmed to respond and adapt to their needs accordingly. In the past, most machine-learning applications operated 'off–line', where a set of training data would be collected and used to fit a statistical model. Nowadays, new techniques are being used to solve real-time inference problems in which multiple streams of data are processed from diverse sources. Statistical analyses are then used to make inferences about the state of the world. For example, when new information is received, probabilities can be updated using Bayes' theorem. This allows machines to learn by reducing the uncertainty of particular variables based on new information being fed into it.

Email management is a mundane example of how machine-learning is starting to be used. The system decides whether or not to notify a person of an incoming message, depending on the nature and content (and therefore the urgency) of

it, and also on the extent to which the person is willing to tolerate a disturbance at that particular moment, which itself depends on the task in which the person is engaged. Contextual information can also be used to make a decision about how relevant the email is, from that person's calendar, from audio and video sensors which monitor the person's focus of attention, and from log files of past user behaviour. Of course, this is for more advanced needs; machine-learning is also used to filter out the much more commonplace and vexing volumes of spam that increasingly assault our mailboxes.

As with previous generations of intelligent systems, however, the success of machine-learning will depend on how accurate the machine's algorithms are at inferring a person's intentions and their actions at a given moment. While people are very much creatures of habit, they can also be highly unpredictable and complex in their needs and desires. For a machine-learning approach to truly succeed, it may well require that both users and computers make their intentions visible to each other: machines indicating to users what they think users want, and users indicating to the machines what they want in turn. Users also like to know how a machine is making its decisions, so ways of communicating how the mechanisms work may be as important as the outcome.

All of this proposes that humans and 'intelligent' machines often need to be able to negotiate, question and answer back – unlike current vehicle navigation systems ('satnav'), whose instructions telling people where to go are sometimes blindly followed by hapless drivers who never question them. If people are prepared to stupidly obey instructions given out by simple computers, this should make us even more concerned about the relationship between people and ever more complex computers as we move toward 2020.

Hard Disks to Digital Footprints

A powerful metaphor that came into prominence in 2007 was the carbon footprint. Suddenly everyone started talking about reducing carbon emissions, from schoolchildren to world leaders, concerned with how we are destroying our planet and what actions can be taken to reduce these footprints. In a similar vein, people are beginning to talk about their ever growing digital footprints. Part of the reason for this is that the limits of digital storage are no longer a pressing issue. It is all around us, costing next to nothing, from ten-a-penny memory sticks and cards to vast digital Internet data banks that are freely available for individuals to store their photos, videos, emails and documents.

Furthermore, huge amounts of information are being recorded and stored daily about people's behaviour, as they walk through the streets, drive their cars and use the Web. While much of this may be erased after a period of time, some is stored more permanently, about which people may be naively unaware. In 2020, it is likely that our digital footprints will be gigantic, distributed everywhere, and in all manner of places and forms.

The decreasing cost and increasing capacity of digital storage also goes hand-in-hand with new and cheap methods for capturing, creating and viewing digital media. The effect on our behaviour has been quite dramatic: people are taking thousands of pictures rather than hundreds each year. They no longer keep them in shoeboxes or stick them in albums but keep them as ever growing digital collections, often online. The use of Web services for photo-sharing is transforming why we take photos by reinventing what we do with them. The production and sharing of digital content has also substantially changed. 'Podcasting' one's home movies on websites like YouTube is becoming a popular pastime, with many people spending more time watching other people's videos than viewing broadcast content.

↑ The Rovio robotic webcam is wirelessly connected to the Internet. It roams around the home providing an audio and video link to keep an eye on family or pets when you're out.

21

Data are also being collected on our behalf or about us for no apparent reason other than because the technology enables it – our digital shadows, if you like. Personal video recorders (PVRs) record TV programmes chosen by the viewer but also automatically store them based on the viewer's viewing profile or other criteria. Similarly, new devices are beginning to appear, such as SenseCam (see 'A Digital Life', below), that can automatically capture all kinds of traces of everyday life, in the form of images, video, conversations and sounds. The same is true for GPS devices which now appear in cars, in mobile phones and even embedded into clothing. All of these are capable of producing and storing large volumes of location data about our comings and goings without any conscious effort on behalf of their owners.

Data are also being deliberately recorded about us by governments, banks and other institutions using technologies such as CCTV, ATMs and phone logging. In the UK, CCTV often generates recorded 'feeds' of conversations and actions, as well as logging exactly where these conversations and actions took place. Some workplaces have meeting rooms that capture the content of and activities around discussions held within them. Many public debates are recorded for posterity by editorialising CCTV: in the UK, the Houses of Parliament are captured on behalf of the nation by the BBC, for example. Most people's financial transactions are logged too, each time a credit card is used. International phone calls from the US are routinely tapped and analysed for suspicious 'terrorist' topics (with advanced word-recognition software allowing interrogators to locate possible conversational threads which are then focused on more attentively).

A strong case in favour of all this logging is its usefulness in combating crime and terrorism. CCTV feeds are being used to discover the aberrant, such as unusual or suspicious behaviours in public settings, and recognition software is beginning to be used for *post hoc* identification of possible suspects.

As this example suggests, simply storing more data without any real purpose is counter to our current culture of preserving for a reason. There has to be a reason for recording, whether it be for posterity or detection. The trade-offs between storing and viewing, or between searching and browsing, will become increasingly important as we move towards 2020. A key concern for the next decades is how we will manage and harness the enormous digital footprints and shadows that are being created by and for everyone.

A digital life: Gordon Bell, a principal researcher at Microsoft, aims to amass an archive of his life by capturing a digital record of all of his interactions with people and machines. To help, he wears a device around his neck called 'SenseCam', developed at Microsoft's research lab in Cambridge, UK. SenseCam is a wearable camera containing sensors that result in a picture being taken whenever there are changes in light, movement and ambient temperature. The result is a digital 'slideshow' of many of the events in everyday life. ➔

Shrink-Wrapped to Mash-Ups

It used to be that only the most highly skilled software developers could write applications, and only professional content producers could provide us with digital data or content that we could use. In the early days of the PC, we all bought our software in shrink-wrapped boxes, spending more money every few years for a new updated version of our operating system, word processor, or spreadsheet application. Likewise, we cut and pasted images for our Powerpoint presentations from 'clip art', and played around with new fonts and features from the software packages we had bought off-the-shelf.

Those days are disappearing fast. The boom in data that we all produce, or 'user-generated content' (UGC), is one of the huge shifts that has changed all of this. Many of us are being more creative than ever before with the digital content we have to hand, whether it be the photos we produce and share, the blogs we write, or the videos we post on YouTube. At the same time, the Internet is making all this content and the tools to deal with it available to everyone. Even better, when we tag our photos and videos with useful information, other people can make use of it in all sorts of ways. Not only can we search for it, but we can cut and paste other people's content, create links to it, and customise it too.

But this isn't all. Add to this all the content that is now available on the Web from the professionals (music, films, photos, and text), and all kinds of data streams can be 'mashed' together. Many 'mash-ups', as they're known, are do-it-yourself applications that merge one kind of data with another. For example, our Facebook page may merge the photos we post, our personal blog, and also contain links to RSS news feeds. More professional mash-ups can combine data from Amazon, eBay, or Google maps to create entirely new applications. For example, Google maps and CraigsList

'New data sources are available to us all the time. We are all fast becoming content producers, publishers and developers as much as we are consumers'

mashed together creates a new Web service that allows people to search for real estate online; BabyNameMap maps the most popular baby names on top of Google maps; Book Burro notices when you're shopping online at Amazon and looks at other online stores to compare prices.

This of course is not just about merging content, but is about creating new kinds of applications, interfaces and experiences for users. It is also about the decentralisation of software development, where non-experts can now participate. The Web is the source of digital materials we can build our experiences around and of the toolkits we can use to build them with. New data sources are available to us all the time, new software is updated, released and accessed at the click of a mouse. We are all fast becoming content producers, publishers and developers as much as we are consumers.

As we approach 2020, we are entering an era where we are much more hands-on with our digital materials, where the world of software is no longer under strict control of developers and engineers, and where we can create a more customised, personalised digital world for ourselves. This will undoubtedly change our notions of ownership as we enter the era of 'home-brewed' applications and services. In the world of 2020, these changes may make us all more in control of our digital destiny, yet at the same time, the rules, regulations and accountability that govern how we live in this digital world may be much harder to pin down.

23

Answer-Phones to Always-On

↑ Twitter Blocks: Twitter is a mini-blogging tool for people to send small text-based nuggets of information to friends, family and co-workers to let them know what they're up to throughout the course of the day. 'Twitter Blocks' provides a way of visualising networks of Twitter friends and the messages they send to each other.

The need to express ourselves and communicate with others is fundamental to what it means to be human. Communication technologies are now letting us stay in touch and talk in more diverse ways than ever. The emergence of new genres of communication in the last few years has not only increased the pace of communication but the amount of it, too. For example, messaging, texting and 'twittering' are on the rise, where groups of friends, families and colleagues keep in touch, engaging in a form of social grooming, like birds or apes, letting each other know on a constant basis what they are doing or have just done. This is a far cry from the early days of discovering one could use the answer-phone to monitor calls before deciding whether to talk to the person at the other end.

The consequences of this shift in how, when and where we communicate are manifold. One is a dramatic increase in the speed of communication which is in turn bound up with the greater expectations of the speed of response. When email replaced paper in business mail, the speed of response to a communication memo or request was expected to be quicker. Now if you own a mobile device that lets you read your email anywhere, there is an expectation you will be responding at all hours of the day, even when on vacation or in the early hours of the morning. The 'texting' culture among teenagers is even more pressurised; not answering within an hour of receiving a text message is considered very uncool. Another example of the quickening of communication is the ability of people to simultaneously deploy IM (instant messaging) with multiple people. This affords a previously impossible level of interaction – though whether continuous partial attention is effective is open to dispute – where dialogues with many different remote people can be maintained all at once.

A downside of being always available and constantly in touch is that it can become addictive. Having access to email and the Web is becoming more commonplace on all phones, and this may increase the spread of the 'disease' of communications addiction. But as with any other addiction, there are ways of dealing with the habit. People increasingly do not feel obliged to answer email on the same day, citing email overload or by being more explicit about being out of touch. There are also numerous self-help books on what it means and how to achieve 'turning off'. Filtering using social metadata is another possibility for people to use to manage their communication and availability better. With this approach, 'who' and 'what' are used as indices to determine whether a message should 'get through' or be left waiting.

Another important set of issues concerns privacy and self-identity. Through their mobile devices, people will not only be always in touch with one another but may be willing to share their mobile digital traces: the locations they pass through, their activities, the profiles of other people they pass on the way and the content they consume and produce. This also suggests that increasingly people will have to worry about personal information getting into the wrong hands. It also raises issues about how we protect the more vulnerable in our society, such as children.

It seems no matter where we go or what we do, 'the network is always there', making us available to the world to make ever more demands. As we move toward 2020, the number of communication channels is likely to continue to diversify and we could be making ourselves always available in even more ways than we are today. These trends could make the old ways of talking, sharing and meeting with others obsolete, or they could give us more choice and offer richer possibilities in how we connect with others and who we connect with.

1.2 Changing Lives

By 2020 more people than ever will be using computing devices of one form or other, be they a retiree in Japan, a schoolchild in Italy or a farmer in Africa. At the same time, each generation will have its own set of demands. 'Silver surfers' will want much more from technology than Web browsing, while the iPod and iPhone generation will be replaced by multiple other new generation Xs. Technology will continue to have an important impact at all stages of life. The way we grow up, live together and grow old is inextricably entwined with computers, whether we like it or not. For each of these stages of life we look at one particular topic in terms of technological developments: what it means to learn, to be a family, and to be healthy and active in old age.

Learning Differently

The nature of learning is changing significantly as more and more technologies are assimilated into children's lives. For example, *how* learning happens (eg taking part in a discussion with people from all over the world on Second Life) and *when* it happens (eg listening to a podcast about pollution while on the school bus home) are diversifying. There are ever more opportunities by which children can access, create and share content with others. Likewise, the nature of teaching is changing, both in terms of how teaching is undertaken and in how its benefits are measured. For example, the way teachers and professors engage with their students during class (eg using interactive whiteboards and tablet PCs to make comments) and after class (eg use of online assessment tools to provide feedback and reports) is very different from the 'chalk and talk' model of the past. What will learning be like in 2020? Will the exercise book and the report card of today even be recognisable? Here, we touch first upon advances made in technology-enhanced learning and, second on new forms of assessment and feedback.

A diverse range of technologies has been developed for educational purposes, from multi-media learning tools to mobile measuring and sensing tools. Interactive whiteboards and WiFi are also becoming more commonplace in schools. As the cost of PCs dramatically drops and cheap mobile phones become more like computers it is likely that the vision of one computer for every child world-wide will be more of a reality by 2020. However, while our schools may be flooded with cheap computers, what really counts is how children and their teachers use them in a learning context. As resources and tools like Wikipedia, Google, Word and PowerPoint become second nature, this is likely to change the way children create, solve problems, express themselves and understand the world. Likewise, the new generation of teachers, who have been brought up with computers themselves, will increasingly be able to customise and incorporate these resources into their lessons.

The Ambient Periscope in action: a student observing pre-recorded videoclips about the habitat while exploring the physical woodland. This was part of a larger project called the Ambient Wood by Yvonne Rogers and colleagues at Sussex University. ⬇

Ubi-learning in the Ambient Wood (University of Sussex): a boy using a digitally augmented probe tool that shows real-time measurements of light and moisture on an accompanying mobile device. →

The new shareable technologies described earlier would seem ideal candidates for supporting innovative forms of collaboration in the classroom, enabling children to learn how to participate in new ways around digital content they are creating. Ubiquitous computing devices are also starting to enter the classroom and the schoolbag. New low-cost sensing technologies are part of chemistry and physics teaching. Even the very youngest children can benefit from computers when they are embedded in objects that encourage hands-on interactive play.

How teachers assess their students is changing, too. Online tools are being developed to make it easier to capture more about students' work in digital form. Whereas, in the past, teachers commonly based their assessment of a learner's progress on the quality of their term paper or science project, today the teacher can see the intermediate steps, the rough drafts, or even the sequence of keystrokes that led to the final product. The capacity of computers to provide ever more finely-grained detailed traces of student behaviour continues to be a major pull in education. A well-rehearsed claim is that teachers can and indeed ought to view digital traces not as merely a tool for spelling and syntax, but as a more

comprehensive and process-focused measure of students' competence and learning. Having access to a student's digital traces may also aid teachers in diagnosing learning difficulties that may have previously been overlooked. This understandably creates new tensions in terms of the overall balance of time a teacher must give to assessing students versus teaching them.

As the trend towards developing more sophisticated technologies to record and assess a pupil's output continues, the way computers are used to support learning and teaching in 2020 may be quite different from today. The impact will not just be in terms of how technology changes the nature of learning and teaching but in other ways, too. It may change, for example, the ways in which parents can become connected to the education process. It may affect the ways in which school invades home and home invades school for children in a culture that is increasingly permeated by connected computer technology.

New Ways of Family Living

Happy Families is a British card game invented in the 1850s that is still played today. The goal is to collect as many complete sets of a four-member family, such as Mr Pint, Mrs Pint, Master Pint, and Miss Pint. Over a century on, this family grouping seems rather quaint. What it means to be part of a family today, let alone a happy family, is quite different. Besides the stereotypical family of 2.4 children, there are many other varieties, including one-parent families and children living together from different marriages. Most family groupings have a desire to stay in touch with each other and to look after one another. At the same time, there are ever-increasing demands on a family member's life, from needing to work or study all day to having to maintain a network of perhaps a hundred online friends.

New technologies are proliferating that enable people to live both their own busy social and working life while enabling them to take an active part in their family life. For example, in the 1980s, AT&T in the United States popularised the slogan 'reach out and touch someone', promoting the use of landline phones as a way of American family members staying in touch with each other. AT&T had noted how the distances that separated family members were getting ever greater. Twenty years on, there is little doubt that the desire to be in touch is as great as ever, though there are many other communication technologies besides the landline phone to support it. The huge uptake of broadband, and the mushrooming of Internet cafes all over the world has enabled many families to stay in touch more frequently than ever before. 'Skyping' has become a popular pastime; even when on holiday family members can talk to one another via a computer-based video connection.

Being in touch is one thing, sharing within families is another. Sharing can be very prosaic, such as sharing photos with family after returning from vacation. In today's world, digital snapshots can be posted on the Web and family members alerted. Being in touch through showing and sharing can bring dispersed family members together. However, it can also highlight exclusions and enmities that before may not have shown themselves.

Family life is also about looking after one's own. Parents often wish to know where their children are and are comforted by knowing they are safe and sound. They also want to know that grandma is looking after herself living alone in her flat. A number of computer applications have been developed to enable family members to keep an eye on one another, from the Family Locator feature on the Disney cell phone (which allows parents to display the location of a child's handset on a map) to devices that can be installed on cars to track their location and speed such as 'Track My Car' from AerComTec. But as such technology becomes pervasive, parents' concern for the whereabouts of their loved ones may easily be perceived as a form of surveillance.

How family occasions occur is also changing. Whereas photos and videos of weddings were sent to distant relatives who could not be there, it is now possible for them to be part of the occasion via video links. The same is true of birthday parties, bar mitzvahs and other rites of passage. Even funerals can now be carried out online, and digital shrines can be constructed to allow relatives to honour the dead, transcending boundaries of both space and time. Digital materials also have important implications for what happens after death. Emptying out the boxes after an aunt's death may no longer be simply a matter of dividing up the jewelry, books and ornaments. By 2020 a person's belongings will include a vast array of digital materials. This raises all sorts of questions about how one sorts through such collections, and whether the relevant social and technology safeguards are in place to allow us access to a loved one's email and other digital belongings once they have passed away. In the next decade or two, we will witness many changes in family life brought about by technology, but also sparking new forms of digital tools. Such changes will of course have a larger impact on societal and ethical issues that is difficult to predict.

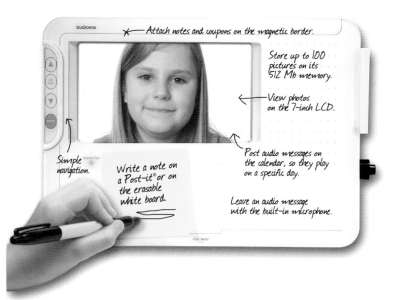

↑ Audiovox's Digital Message Center is designed to be attached to the refrigerator, letting families scribble digital notes and leave audio and video messages for each other.

New Ways of Growing Older

By 2020 there will be far more elderly people as a proportion of the total population. Computer technologies are being developed to support them in old age, from health-monitoring devices to memory aids. Unlike previous generations, those growing old will be familiar with using computers and mobile phones. Hence, the need to design computer applications for old people who have not used email or the Web will no longer be a major concern. But staying healthy is becoming central to many people as they learn more about their bodies. People of all ages are regularly checking their body functions, such as cholesterol levels and heart rate. More monitoring devices will come into the market that will allow people to monitor themselves in new ways, and this in turn will alter the balance between what they understand about their own health and the information offered to them by medical experts. Online support communities will increase where people can upload their personal health data or send photos of what they have eaten and a log of their activities to online doctors who can give them up-to-date and personalised assessments. Such digital records of bodily and psychological health may also become resources for new ways of sharing and documenting the medical travails of older life, allowing for more customised and reassuring health care.

But it is also the case that middle-aged people, who are now in their 50s and 60s, are likely to still feel young and fit in their 70s and 80s, owing to their healthier lifestyles. Applications are being designed for their leisure, such as social networking and gaming sites. This trend can already be observed in the percentage of active users over 45 (11.52% in 2007) in Second Life, and in the emergence of virtual bowling leagues using Nintendo's Wii system.

As people get older they will also want to remain active in ways previous generations did not. They will want to continue to be part of the workplace, to drive and to travel the world. There are currently restrictions in several countries that prevent them from doing this. For example, many car rental companies in Europe do not allow anyone over 70 to drive their cars (for insurance purposes). But this is likely to change as people remain mentally alert and more computer-aided devices are placed in cars to make driving easier and safer. As a case in point, automatic parking aids are starting to become available to help people who find it hard to see behind them.

Part of the reason for this change has to do with the fact that the retiree of 2020 will have spent a lifetime growing up with computer systems, having used them in their jobs, entertained themselves through the Web and experienced many of the 'IT revolutions' first hand. They will also expect and be capable of using new technologies as they come on the market. They will want to use them to stay connected to society, work colleagues, friends and children. They will want them to support their health and well-being. And as they get older still, friends and family may want computers to keep an eye on their aging family members. Technology in 2020 will alter not only the day-to-day experience of being old, but it will change how we regard ourselves, how we regard aging, and how we see the place of the elderly in society.

Sony's EyeToy being played by grandpa. A camera on the TV projects his image on to the playing screen, allowing him to interact with the game using arm movements and gestures. ➜

1.3 Changing Societies

Governments are using computers and, in particular, the Web, in more ways than ever. They do so both to inform their citizens (eg sickness benefits, visa requirements) and to gather information about them (eg returning online tax forms, voting online at an election). Cameras take pictures of car number plates to automatically bill owners for anything from road taxes and tolls to congestion charges. Speed cameras flash as you whiz past them, signalling that a speeding ticket will be landing on your doormat in a few days. Identity cards and passports have increasing amounts of digital information embedded in them that can be read at passport controls. Opinions about what information governments need and ought to have, and what citizens ought reasonably to provide are changing. In many ways, technology is making the relationship between government and the individual more complex, not least because it is often difficult to know how much information is being gathered, how it is being used, and who has control of it.

← A man in Cape Town, South Africa, selling mobile phones. In 2007, 77% of Africans had a mobile phone, while only 11% had computer access.

This holds true at a world-wide level: in some ways the world is more uniformly governed and this is being achieved through computing; in other ways it is not and this is sometimes because of computing. For example, one agency governs the issuance of addresses for the World Wide Web. As it happens, this is a US-based institution. This means that wherever one is, whatever one wants to do, the name one uses is governed by an institution that governs us all. By contrast, how individual sites on the Web get indexed is partly a matter of concern to the creator of a site, since the choice of indexing terms is up to them. But it is partly also to do with a technical property of the search engine that is used to locate that site. The bottom line is that global connectivity is no real indication that one set of rules will govern us all.

Just as governments are using new technologies to change how they do business, so too are the public using them to change their governments. The use of mobile phones to mobilise demonstrations at G8 meetings is a recent case. As famous is the 'coup de text' that toppled President Estrada of the Philippines in 2001. What happens on the world wide stage is now affecting what happens locally. Global communications mean that the fate of individuals subject to one form of governance can have an effect, in real time, elsewhere, on individuals subject to very different political circumstances. One consequence of this is that internal and foreign affairs are subjected more to the media glare. Football games and demonstrations, terrorist acts and peaceful elections, all these and more are viewed through the lens of the TV newsreel, the blog, and YouTube.

All of these changes are not just true for the 'developed' or Western world. The availability of cheap computers and mobile phones has lowered the entry point for these devices onto the market, enabling poorer nations to

'By 2020, there will be very few people left on the planet who do not have access to a mobile phone'

participate too. In Africa, the cellular market grew by around 60% between 2004 and 2007. While only 11% of the population had access to desktop computers in 2007, 77% have mobile phones. Furthermore, analysts have predicted that over 220 million people in India will be playing games on their mobiles by 2009. By 2020, there will be very few people left on the planet who do not have access to a mobile phone.

One obvious consequence of this is that the mobile will become an increasingly important platform for computer applications for economically growing countries. This highlights the fact that technologies such as mobile phones are no longer used by a single group of people or in a single location. Computers increasingly span the globe and are being used by many differing cultures. This broadening may bring us together, but it may also highlight our differences. For example, many of the people who have been acquiring mobiles in Africa are not computer-literate. Some are also unfamiliar with the concept of information hierarchies, making it hard for them to understand hierarchical menus. Concepts that are familiar to their culture and the local ways of doing things may instead become more common-place as we move toward 2020.

As computing takes hold across the globe, new technologies will show different emergent patterns of use in other cultures, and will be appropriated in new ways by them. Technologies will not only be a sign of a changing world, but will accelerate those changes. How we understand these different cultural values and accept them as we move towards 2020 will be an issue for debate and reflection, and will offer up many new opportunities for research and design.

The next thing in the digital economy? Visa Micro Tag does away with the need to swipe a credit card or give your card to the cashier. Just wave the tag in front of a secure reader and the payment is made. ➔

Summary

Computers have played a massive role in changing the way we live over the last couple of decades. They are no longer possessions of the privileged but are rapidly becoming inexpensive, everyday commodities. They have evolved from being isolated machines to globally interconnected devices. Not only has access to computers vastly increased, but the ways we interact with them and materials used for computer devices have changed too. All of this means that computers can now be interwoven with almost every aspect of our lives. As we move towards 2020, so the extent of these changes will increase. By 2020, it may not be possible to realise all of our goals, ambitions and aspirations without using a computer or computing in one way or another. This binding of computing to our daily activities will in turn affect our values, goals and aspirations.

2 Transformations in Interaction

Part 1 described the many kinds of changes that have happened in our relationship with computers. This Part reflects on these, summarising five major transformations that are dramatically affecting how we interact with computing technology as we move towards 2020. These range from how we understand and design interaction, to the nature of their impact on society. For each one, we highlight the opportunities and issues these transformations raise, specifying some of the important concerns that future research and development will need to address. Many of the challenges will be different from before, as will the questions we should be asking. We need to look at the world differently, and start to construct a new research agenda.

ART+COM's artistic installation called Duality, located at the exit ➜ of a metro station in Tokyo. Passers-by provoke virtual ripple effects with their footsteps, as if walking across a pond.

2.1 Human Values in the Face of Change

The changes we have described in Part 1 – in computers, individual lives and society – can be viewed as examples of five major transformations which are irrevocably altering the relationship we have with computers.

The first has to do with how the proliferation and embedding of technology has reshaped the way digital devices are presented to us, the interface. Computing no longer has a single interface, but rather many different ones. Some are created by computers encroaching ever more on our own personal space, even being embedded within us. Others are produced by computers moving away and disappearing into the richness and complexity of the world around us. In other words, this transformation is **the end of interface stability**, almost making old notions of the 'interface' obsolete. What an interface might be, where it is, what it allows a user to do, even whether there is one at all are, now, all questions for a future-looking HCI.

Second, changes in how we live with and use technology have resulted in us becoming ever more dependent upon computing. It's not simply that we use computing to, say, create our work documents or our tax returns; computing now underpins almost every aspect of our lives, from shopping to travel, from work to medicine. At the same time, computers are becoming more sophisticated and autonomous, increasing our reliance on them. Thus, a further transformation has to do with what one might call **the growth of techno-dependency**.

Third, the increasing importance of communication technologies in our private and public lives has tied us together in new ways. At issue here is more than the fact that we find it easier and quicker to, say, email one another rather than write a handwritten letter; today (and even more so in the future) we will spend more time, and devote more effort, to being in touch with each other. In addition to keeping us closer to those

we care about, digital connectivity also has the power to mobilise crowds and respond to events in global ways. This transformation is **the growth of hyper-connectivity**.

Fourth, our desire to be in touch is equalled by our desire to capture more information about our lives and our doings. With increasing technological capacity to capture and store more data and the related reduction in the cost of such storage, what it means to record, why we record and what we do with the collected materials is changing. This is happening at a personal level, and also at the level of government, institutions and agencies. We call this transformation **the end of the ephemeral**.

Finally, the proliferation and appropriation of new kinds of digital tools by people from all walks of life signals **the growth of creative engagement** through technology. This is not confined to artists or media professionals, but all kinds of people, whatever their trade or stage in life. Important developments are occurring in the world of science – and thus how computer-based tools are augmenting human reasoning. This transformation is affecting all of us, enabling us to work, play and express ourselves in new ways.

Each of these five transformations impacts on the way we view interaction and design, and raises far-reaching questions for us all. In the face of all this change, though, some important things will remain the same. Above all, the characteristics that make us essentially human will continue to be manifest in our relationship with technology. People will still wish to be part of families, to stay connected with friends, to educate their children, to care for each other when they are unwell, and to grow old safely and in comfort. Technology, digital or otherwise, is the enabler for all of these things rather than the focus. Shifts in computing are therefore not at the forefront of people's concerns. What does concern them is how technologies can support the

'The characteristics that make us human will continue to be manifest in our relationship with technology'

things that matter to them in their daily lives – the things they value.

By *human values*, we mean the ideas we all hold about what is desirable in different situations, societies and cultural contexts. They guide our actions, judgements and decisions, and are fundamental to what makes us human. There are many that we can all agree on, such as taking care of loved ones, being active and healthy, and developing and maintaining friendships. Others may be more contentious, such as the desire to control one's surroundings and relationships, the quest for spiritual salvation and the pursuit of sexual gratification. Whether or not we hold a particular set of values to be true for ourselves, they are concerns that are nonetheless more broadly important to us, and that we, as humans, orient to. Whether technology helps us in attaining what we desire in our lives or not, there is no doubt it affects the ways in which we pursue our goals and aspirations, and the ways in which we see ourselves and others.

We propose that 'being human' in our relationship with technology means that we need to bring to the fore and better understand human values and make them central to how we understand and design for a changing world. But these human values need to be understood against the backdrop of the major transformations we describe. The rest of this section will discuss each of these in more detail. For each transformation, we look at how it impacts on the way we view interaction and design. We also examine the kinds of human values that are important to consider, and raise some of the broader issues these transformations will provoke.

2.2 The End of Interface Stability

When we consider the digital world we inhabit, the sheer proliferation of ways in which we encounter digital technology is astounding. The last few decades have seen not only an enormous growth in the number of devices but also an almost explosive diversification in the nature of these devices as they have entered every aspect of our lives. We face a future where we will need to live with an ever growing and always changing set of interconnected digital devices. Some of these will be close to us and even embedded within us, while others will be invisibly built into our surrounding environment. How these technologies are manifest in the world and the extent to which they and their interactive capabilities are noticeable to us will be equally diverse. We need to understand and design for interaction in a world where the notion of an interface is no longer easily defined, stable or fixed. Here, we consider how this flux will affect the boundary between computational devices: between computers and people, and between computers and the physical world.

The shifting boundary between computers and humans

Our relationship with computers has altered dramatically. Where the interface or point of contact with computers now resides (the boundary between us and machines) and the extent to which it is visible to us is now no longer as clear as when we interacted at the desktop or the terminal. One trajectory is inward, moving the boundary closer to us and making our interaction with digital systems more intimate in nature. For example, we now carry in our pockets and our handbags multiple points of contact to a computational infrastructure, such as a mobile phone, iPod or BlackBerry. With the shift to medical monitoring and embedded bio-sensing devices this is likely to get closer still. Indeed, it may be difficult to define the boundary at all when devices are embedded within us.

Electronic sensing jewelry (a concept from Philips Design) is based on stretchable, flexible electronic substrates that integrate energy supply, sensors, actuators, and display. By changing colour or even shape according to your mood, it explores how wearable technology can be playful, sensual, mood-affected, bio-activity stimulated. ➔

The transformation in interface boundaries relative to our own bodies raises many new questions about how we might interact with new technologies. As the boundary moves closer to us, so the focus of the interaction and how it will affect their own personal experience needs to be better understood by the individual. As these devices become part of us, it raises issues about what defines an individual, and whether embedded devices are part of that definition.

The issues are more complicated than this, however. Personal, intimate devices can be networked and therefore can interact with other people and other devices within the wider environment. So we need to consider the spectrum of use, ranging from private and personal interaction at one end to public and aggregated interaction at the other. We can now receive unwanted BlueToothed files on our mobile phones. It is not long before personal devices might be detected by billboards, shopfronts, pavements and walls as we walk along them, delivering customised information or messages to us. At any one moment this means we may be simultaneously interacting with multiple boundaries, some under our control and some not. This will cause shifts in what we perceive as personal space, and what is shared.

How do human values affect the interface boundaries? For example, the desire for vitality and independence as we grow older might motivate us to place medical devices close to or even within our bodies. But how does this affect other human values, such as the need to define our own identity? If computers are embedded within us, are they then part of that identity? And what about sharing that data with others? If others have access to our most intimate data, do we then feel a loss of the independence we might seek? Likewise, if the boundary between us and embedded devices is invisible, how important is it that we

← The last five years have seen an explosion in the number of digital hearing aids on the market. They are a good example of wearable computing and of the trend toward intimate, embedded technology.

manage and control that boundary? These are all issues that we will increasingly have to deal with in future.

Questions for interaction and design
- How will we know what computational resources are available within us and how these will interact with resources around us?
- What interaction techniques are appropriate if embedded devices have no explicit or recognisable interface?
- Will more intimate devices mean old concepts of 'the interface' become obsolete and irrelevant in the future?

Questions of broader impact
- Will the embedding of bio-sensing devices be acceptable only for cases of extreme frailty or illness or for other purposes too?
- Should the bodily functions of people be allowed to be monitored without their awareness or permission?
- How should we access and control information from intimate, embodied devices?

37

↑ **Another playful piece of technology is the History Tablecloth, by the Interaction Research Studio (Goldsmiths College, University of London). It is designed to cover a kitchen or dining-room table. When objects are left on the table, the cloth starts to glow beneath them, creating a halo that expands very slowly. When items are removed, the glow fades quickly.**

The shifting boundary between computers and the everyday world

Just as the interface between people and computers is radically altering, so, too, is the boundary between computational technology and the objects and surfaces in the everyday world. In future, a computer is more likely to be embedded in furniture, rooms, cars, doors, clothing, and packaging than in a recognisable 'box'. There are two trajectories at play here. One is moving devices into everyday artefacts and objects, augmenting them with new sensing, communication and computational capabilities. The other is moving the devices into the surrounding landscape, augmenting it with interactive capabilities that respond to changes and activities within them.

The interaction between digital technologies and the physical objects they are embedded in will change existing forms of interaction. This link will become less clear in a world where we relate to technologies via physical artefacts that may look and feel like everyday, familiar objects, but which have some kind of digital impact. We will need new conceptual models and metaphors of how best to support and control these new forms of more 'natural' but paradoxically less obvious forms of interaction. For example, what will replace the canonical 'undo', 'cut and paste', 'save' and 'copy' actions of the desktop in the world of physical-digital artefacts? Research is needed to determine what will be the most natural, efficient and socially accepted means of controlling such interactions.

The new relationships between digital devices and the world will bring to the fore a host of human values that hitherto have not been considered in relation to technology – many of which are manifest in the nature of the world we inhabit. For example, familiar physical artefacts and objects that provide us with reassurance and comfort are something that we all understand. The physical world we inhabit and the artefacts we use in our world are associated with a medley of personal, social and cultural values. They will shape our understanding of new technologies within it. Consider the technologies we might place in a church, a museum, a railway station or a stadium. Which kinds of displays and interactive technologies and how they are placed in them will differ considerably.

As new forms of 'natural' and 'indirect' interaction develop, the consequences of their use in the public sphere raise significant issues for society. For one, it is not clear how social interaction will be managed in such settings and how these, in turn, will impinge upon society's values. Shared values need to be considered in terms of how spaces might be designed to reflect a community of users. The deployment of large-scale sensing systems, such as traffic monitoring and RFID tags in supply chains, have already highlighted the need for debate on the appropriate and socially acceptable use of digital technologies that sense our actions through our interactions with the physical world.

Questions for interaction and design
- How should new interaction techniques be merged with pre-existing skills dealing with everyday objects?
- If everything we see, touch or walk past is interactive, how will we know and how can we control that interaction?
- How useful are conventional definitions of 'use' and 'users'?

Questions of broader impact
- How acceptable will indirect interaction be to society? For example, will it be acceptable to provide invisible interactive services in public toilets, on the beach, or in the wilderness?
- Will people need to always be provided with an indication they have initiated an interaction?
- Should people be allowed to opt in or out of a more connected interactive world?

Living in a computational ecosystem

Computers will not only pervade our everyday world, but they will increasingly work together either in intended or unintended ways, often independently of human involvement. Sometimes this will be for our benefit, but at other times to our detriment. When devices are interconnected, it may be more difficult for people to understand how they work. Moreover, technologies are likely to give rise to emergent properties that are not only unpredictable but difficult to diagnose. Evolving computational ecosystems shaped by the merging of human and computing entities will result, likewise, in ever more complex scenarios of use. We have international banking systems that allow us to use our credit cards anywhere. But there are automatic security systems which can inhibit this use, for instance. Furthermore, they are likely to produce unexpected effects that are aggregated across multiple places of contact and a dynamic changing infrastructure.

Although people may value surprise and unpredictability in some walks of life (such as in art or in games), in others, it is unwelcome. There are many systems we depend on to help us get from one place to another, to get our work done, and to keep us safe. Will increasing levels of complexity undermine our sense of safety and security in the world? Will our lack of understanding make us less confident about living in an increasingly digital world? As part of understanding the complexity, we need to be able to find ways of presenting it to people in a form they can make sense of and act upon.

The unconstrained and potentially unbounded nature of the new computational ecosystems makes it ever more difficult to reason about the consequences of interaction. So, how will people cope, especially when things do not appear to work in the way intended? It is difficult enough when we can't diagnose why our home broadband network has stopped working. What happens when our computational networks become larger and more inter-connected with others? How does one start to understand where the problems lie? Who is responsible? One approach is to develop visualisations and other representations that can make the workings of the ecosystems more visible and understandable to those who have become part of them.

The emergence of increasingly complex computational ecosystems will also have significant impact on our views of society and technology. The ability to rapidly disseminate information globally and to make complex inferences from aggregated data collection will be an increasing cause of concern among civil liberty groups. New forms of legislation will be needed, together with a range of new sense-making tools that will enable policy-makers to understand the unfolding complexity that is emerging.

Questions for interaction and design
- How do we enable people to understand the complexity of new ecosystems of technologies and the consequences of interacting with them?
- What happens when things stop working or break down in these new ecosystems?
- How should information be passed between interconnected devices and how will increasingly pressing concerns, such as security and privacy, be managed?

Questions of broader impact
- How will we understand the complexity of our interactions sufficiently to control them and prohibit actions that are considered unacceptable to society?
- How can we legislate for local interactions having potentially global effects?
- Who will be responsible and accountable for preventing breakdowns, fixing problems and protecting society from the unplanned and undesirable consequences of complex ecosystems?

2.3 The Growth of Techno-Dependency

As new technologies become more interwoven into our everyday activities, we will become more dependent on the new capabilities they provide, often to the point where we will find it hard to imagine how things could be done any other way. It is now an ordinary event to visit an automatic bank machine. Most of us would find it both unusual and inconvenient to have to visit a bank and interact with a human teller in order to withdraw money. Likewise, most of us would feel both affronted and frustrated if our personal computers were taken away and we were suddenly forced to use an old-fashioned typewriter to create documents. We are so used to working with computers to undertake everyday tasks that we tend only to think about them when they break down or are unavailable. Similarly, we are so dependent on complex computers in most aspects of our lives that we barely give them a second thought. For example, we routinely fly on planes that are entirely dependent on the sophistication of the underlying computer systems rather than the inherent skills of the pilot. Our dependency on computer technologies will become increasingly the norm over the next decade.

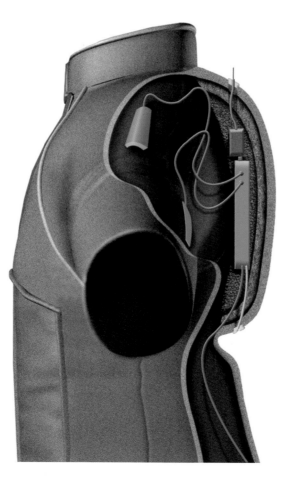

I-Garment is developing full-bodied smart garments – to be worn by fire-fighters and the like – that monitor and transmit the location and vital signals of its wearer (such as body temperature and heartbeat). ➜

Living in an increasingly technology-reliant world

Each generation acquires a new set of technologies in addition to the older ones they have become dependent on. Many of today's children have grown up with the Internet at their fingertips, instant availability through mobile phones, access to vast archives of their personal music and photographs, and video and TV on demand. They also take for granted older technologies such as calculators, word processors, and email. But what happens when the Internet or a mobile network provider goes offline for a period of time? When the national electricity grid goes down, people bring candles out and read books. When networks go down, people become suddenly aware of their dependence, or even addiction, to email and the Web.

Technological dependence raises a number of fundamental questions for how we design and understand computers. An important set of issues has to do with the skill-sets that change over generations, and also those that will increasingly disappear. Designers of technology need to take into account what their target users already know and what they will expect. At the same time, other key skills that previous generations have taken for granted may become obsolete. With the uptake of calculators, educationalists became increasingly worried that children's mental arithmetic skills were disappearing. In 2020, what other kinds of basic skills might go? We are already hearing arguments that the new world of digital media augurs badly for children's attention span and their ability to read and concentrate.

Technological dependence interacts with other fundamental human values. For example, it is also the case that the more we depend on technologies to carry out or mediate our everyday activities the more we will need to trust them to do so. How does such blanket trust develop? Will people in the future be able to adapt to situations where access and use of technologies cannot be taken for granted? Is this increasing reliance on technology a healthy state of affairs for society? How does this weigh up with our natural curiosity to understand the facilities we use in order to trust them? One potential downside to all of this is a loss of independence and self-reliance, and a lack of depth and breadth of understanding about how the world works. If we are not careful, undermining these values may make the world of 2020 a much less rewarding world to live in.

Finally, technological reliance is different the world over, and there are understandable concerns about the global digital divide. If access to computing technology will mean much more than owning a PC and having Internet access, what will be the key technologies that some parts of the world will require? Part of the answer here is not simply economic. The bulk of the world's people now use mobile phones as their primary computer, with all sorts of implications for its functionality and design. A mobile is not and never will be a PC-in-the-hand; they are essentially different things, irrespective of the processing power they contain. A mobile offers an emphasis on communication, portability and even wearability in ways that a PC never can, while a PC can afford ease of document creation. Besides this, the metaphors used to design both mobiles

'The more we depend on technologies to carry out or mediate our everyday activities, the more we will need to trust them to do so'

and PCs have tended to emphasise individual actions despite the fact that in some parts of the world computer systems are used by communities. Villages in India provide the most obvious example of this, but similar communal interaction with computers doubtless occurs elsewhere too. In short, solutions to the digital divide will need to include novel approaches to design as well as cost.

Questions for interaction and design
- Will there be ever-increasing expectations for better and faster technologies and what does this mean for the new technologies we design?
- What will be the taken-for-granted technologies in 2020 and how might this alter the skill-sets and understandings of future generations?
- How do we design technologies to help people cope in an increasingly technology-dependent world when the infrastructures break down, devices malfunction or get lost?

Questions of broader impact
- If numeric skills can be supplemented by the ubiquitous presence of calculators, what other skills will become potentially obsolete? Should society be concerned about this?
- Is technology to be blamed for accidents and disasters or are designers and developers held responsible?
- As society grows ever dependent on technology and the interaction underpinning this, who is accountable?

Living with increasingly clever computers

As computer systems become more sophisticated, they have also become more independent. More are beginning to make choices and decisions on our behalf. For example, popular recommender systems give guidance on what we might like to do or buy. As computers become more autonomous they also have become increasingly present in our world. 'Clever' computers can now clean our floors, help us find our way, and are even beginning to become our pets and companions. These developments raise fundamental questions about how we should live with them, what our relationships should be, together with larger social and ethical issues of responsibility and accountability.

What might be an appropriate kind of relationship? Rather than instructing or issuing commands, it may mean designing interactions to be more like human-human conversations. But will people be happy talking to their robots as if they were pets or even people? This question has been around for many years but will become more pressing as clever computers become more of a reality.

And, what will be the kinds of tasks we feel happy to let clever computers do? For example, will we trust driverless transportation in the future to move our children to and from school? Likewise, will we trust computers to undertake medical intervention? Computers already play a major role in safety-critical systems such as air traffic control and nuclear power plants, but do we feel it is acceptable that they also begin to take on more social roles in society? In Japan, some are now proposing that robots be developed as companions for the elderly. If this is acceptable, how should we design them so that we do not completely abdicate responsibility? We need to decide. We also need to consider the consequences of a world inhabited by independent computers that we have less control over. A sense of control over our own environment is a key human value. Will clever computer systems undermine or enhance this?

Part of this sense of control is related to how we account for our activities. We treat being responsible for what we do as a measure of sophistication and knowledge; this is why children and adolescents are not subject to criminal proceedings in the same way as adults. Such systems of accountability are not confined to matters of criminality of course but also suffuse our professional and personal actions. This, in turn, drives many broader societal relations and understandings. As computing takes on more roles in our activities and as our environment becomes constructed and controlled by computers that we might not even be aware of, these systems of etiquette, accountability and responsibility will be affected. How will we know that this is happening? Who will judge what the consequences might be?

Questions for interaction and design
- What will be an appropriate style of interaction with clever computers?
- What kinds of tasks will be appropriate for computers, and when should humans be in charge?
- How can clever computers be designed to be trustworthy, reliable and acting in the interests of their owners?

Questions of broader impact
- To what extent will society allow clever computers the trust we currently give to trained and qualified professionals?
- Is it proper to assign what used to be human roles to computers? For example, is it acceptable to allow robots to be companions for the elderly or infirm?
- Who will we hold accountable when things go wrong with autonomous systems?
- What are the implications for society of having clever computers reasoning and acting on our behalf?

2.4 The Growth of Hyper-Connectivity

The ability to communicate through multiple interactive devices will continue to grow and diversify as we approach 2020. We are already starting to see a transformation from the 90s communication technologies that resulted in most people being always-on to more extreme forms of hyper-connectivity in the 00s through increasingly more diverse sets of communication channels and media. But what are the implications of such an explosive and rapid growth in connectivity to individuals and society at large? And what will it be like in 2020?

Living in a more socially connected world

We now connect at greater distances and over longer time-frames with our friends and family than ever before. We reach each other more of the time wherever we are, and are available for contact any place, any time. We are also making new friends and building new forms of relationships, many of whom we may only ever meet through digital channels. This is changing the way we build and maintain our relationships at work, home and play. The boundaries between the office and home, and between work and play are dissolving. It is perfectly normal now for people to be emailing their work colleagues in the early hours while playing a game of online poker with people they have never met. Traditional, socially accepted conventions and etiquette governing how we communicate, when we communicate, whom we communicate with and what else we are doing are rapidly disappearing. New ones are replacing them but it seems that anything goes now. For example, students feel it is perfectly acceptable to email their professors with excuses for late assignments using informal text slang. Professors, however, may feel differently. We need to examine how the rules of conversation at work, school, among friends and family are being transformed by the proliferation of communication technologies.

Mobile phones can help to isolate us in a crowd. Alternatively, they can mobilise the masses, for better or worse. →

Hyper-connectivity also raises a number of fundamental issues for understanding and designing interaction. The need to attend to multiple demands will increase with spiralling overheads. Currently, we are used to managing demands by changing physical location (we are either at work or not) or managing our time (we spend time with our families at the weekend). However, hyper-connectivity undermines both these resources. As a result we will need to discover new ways of managing multiple points of interaction that vary in terms of purpose, scope and scale.

The human values of community and connection will be tested: they are both supported and undermined by the new waves of communication technologies. The need to be connected to others and avoid isolation drives not only the development of more kinds of communication devices, but motivates and shapes our use of them. However, set against this is the basic human need to have time for independence and quiet reflection. There is therefore an inherent tension in the extent and level of connection we find acceptable. The danger is that we will end up in a state of extreme connectivity that will invade the human need to disconnect and spend time on our own, or with close friends and family.

The shift towards hyper-connectivity provokes fundamental questions about the core elements of our society. Previously stable and fixed divisions have now become more permeable. If we carry a mobile email device, the division between work and home starts to blur. When we are members of online communities that span the globe, the notion of neighbourhood becomes different. We are in a time where conventions and norms are being radically reshaped, and where we are defining how we manage our interactions in both physical and social spaces. These will have major consequences both for our well-being and the well-being of those we care about. Parents are rightly worried about how their children connect to others through the Internet – a unique problem of the 21st century. It is becoming more of a challenge to do the right thing, and provide safety nets that in the past might have seemed more straightforward.

Questions for interaction and design
- How can technology help us manage our availability to others, and what information should be made available?
- What new codes of etiquette will come into play? How much should new technologies and services be designed to take these into account?
- How can new communication technologies be designed to let people know that the people they meet digitally really are who they say they are?

Questions of broader impact
- What are the appropriate social structures and practices needed to help us live in a connected world and how do they relate to our current practices?
- What impact will large-scale social networks have upon us, our families and friends, and society at large?
- How should we properly police a connected society for the benefit of all without the technologies of connection becoming misused?

Being part of a digital crowd

Digital technologies are not only everpresent, but they allow remote events to have an immediate impact upon us. In today's world, we anticipate receiving notification of world events immediately. We now routinely see images captured on mobile phones spread across the world in minutes. We are also starting to see our actions and activities having global influence in terms of our abilities to motivate and mobilise the population to respond to particular events. We are becoming part of the digital crowd, where our local actions can have widespread and potentially global interactive effect. However, we understand little of how this transformation is taking place and how we might design new technologies to facilitate and keep it in check.

We have seen the power of digital technology for many years in terms of how it allows the sharing and sometimes flaring up of opinion. Newsgroups and email have long played a role in dissemination of public opinion. We are now seeing more compelling examples of 'smart mobs', where people are able to self-organise on a massive scale through technology. This impromptu, ad hoc use of technology can be used for organising protests, taking mass action, and galvanising public opinion behind a cause. But likewise it can be used to stalk celebrities, spread misinformation, and provoke civil unrest. As we approach 2020, there may be many ways in which the infrastructure, nature of the tools, and interaction will need to change to accommodate and help manage this transformation.

The values of community and shared identity lie at the core of a sense of the digital crowd. Our desires to be accepted and part of a common value system motivate the ways in which we are already seeing technology being used. However, it is worth noting that the difference between 'crowd' and 'mob' may be small; understanding how one or the other is manifest is important to the stability of society. For example, will we face distributed online protest? The digital crowd is likely to play a

'The digital crowd is likely to play a more influential role in shaping the human values of the future'

more influential role in shaping the human values as opinions are voiced and information shared via digital means. Will this undermine our current set of human values or enhance them?.

Another concern is the extent to which the voice of the digital crowd reflects a real reaction or overreaction. Consider, for example, the number of times that existing Internet technologies are viewed as promoting 'extreme' views. It is a concern that is already becoming pressing for many governments. For example, in the UK, the Ministry of Defence has prohibited military personnel from access or contribution to blogs while on active service duty.

Questions for interaction and design
- What are the patterns of interaction that emerge as local action sparks interaction and reaction on a mass scale?
- How can we deal with potential negative effects of instant and widespread dissemination of information or misinformation?
- How do we design tools and infrastructures to allow digital crowds to form without overloading the infrastructure and allowing phenomena to be managed appropriately?

Questions of broader impact
- How can technologies be used to effectively assemble and mobilise groups of people to tackle global problems?
- How should the global impact of interaction be handled and what impact will increased connectivity with remote world events have?
- What is the role of government and legislation in shaping the acceptable behaviour of digital crowds?

2.5 The End of the Ephemeral

Another major transformation that is taking place is our expanding digital footprint. More and more ephemeral aspects of our lives, which used only to be stored in human memory, are being recorded as digital 'memories'. We now live in a world where our interactions and activities are often on the record. CCTV cameras record our movements in public spaces, while barcodes or RFID tags on products record our shopping transactions. Our online activities through Web interaction, blogs and social software are also increasingly open to both explicit and implicit archiving. Furthermore, many of these digital records are being indexed in one form or another, allowing them to be readily retrieved at a later date. What does this mean for individuals and society?

Managing expanding digital footprints

Expanding digital footprints have already started to challenge the prevailing views of privacy and ethics. New laws are needed to ensure people have the protection rights they desire over their own and other's personal data. There is also a need to investigate new forms of authentication, security and personal identification and to explore what this means at the level of interaction. This will become ever more pressing as we move toward 2020.

The growth and management of our digital footprints highlight significant differences between human and computational views of interaction. Recollecting and forgetting is bound up with the initial encoding of human experience. This is quite different from the more rigid and mechanistic way in which digital information is typically recorded. Memories tend to fade over time and change through interpretation. Digital records are more static, tending to persist in a stable form. Many systems are built on the assumption that the more data we capture the better. In contrast, humans place great value on being selective in what they remember. It is important that we sometimes forget and that we can rely on the tendency of others to forget our past actions and activities too. But digital records are merciless: a silly prank

captured on a mobile phone and then uploaded to a photo-sharing site may haunt someone for the rest of their lives in a way it never did before. Will it be possible for people to delete digital memories captured by others? Now that there are digital tools that can record everything we say or do, how will this affect our own abilities and ways of remembering?

Digital footprints obviously raise new challenges for how we design technologies. But they also need to be understood as a social phenomenon. Memories help us honour the past and shape our sense of identity. How we might share our memories with family, friends and the wider world lies at the heart of how we wish to be seen by others and how we share our experiences. Today, we still can exercise some control over what personal data we reveal to others, and the different ways in which we might present it to friends, family and work colleagues. But in the future we are likely to have less control over our digital records. This fact, coupled with the persistence of our personal data in many domains may well have more far-reaching societal impact than we even begin to imagine.

Questions for interaction and design
- What tools and technologies are needed to effectively manage vast quantities of personal data?
- How can the privacy and security of digital footprints be ensured to prevent misuse but at the same time allow them to be shared with others when needed?
- How do people find out about their digital footprint and what tools should be provided?

Questions of broader impact
- How should society manage the storage and access of human data ethically and responsibly?
- Will people have the right to have information removed from their digital footprints?
- What are the legal implications of a growing digital footprint that maintains a record of our present and past?

Living in an increasingly monitored world

In addition to the personal data we generate and collect, governments, institutions and agencies will have more access to both real time and archived data reflecting the activities of large groups of people. CCTV cameras already capture and monitor behaviour in public places for crime-prevention and traffic-management purposes. The flow and speed of traffic on our road systems are monitored for many different purposes. Our activities on the Internet can be used to target advertising. Likewise, schools, hospitals and other public or private institutions can monitor, capture, and analyse the behaviour of their client or customer base. We are entering an era where the activities and actions of the public at large are increasingly being captured, processed and used as a basis for judgement by others, often without their knowledge or consent.

A concern is the level of awareness people have when being monitored by technology and whether it affects them. Should they be informed of the information that is being captured about them, who has access to it and how it is being used? To what extent do we need to design technology that allows people both control and feedback about what kinds of data are being monitored? The current asymmetric nature of the interaction between those being observed and those doing the observing highlights concerns about the use and abuse of monitoring technology. If we are uncertain about when and where information is being captured about us, to whom it is available and for what purpose, then we are likely to feel our privacy is infringed and may even feel threatened by the ability of others to misuse this information. For example, digital technologies and the ability to edit closed circuit TV footage and photos leave us all open to being misrepresented, and to libellous actions by others.

The way in which we value security is primarily around increased monitoring, such as the desire to safeguard our streets and public places. At a more personal level, information captured through digital devices about people's activities (such as their location) can provide comfort to others. It can, for example, reassure us of the well-being of our loved ones, such as children or elderly relatives. However, the asymmetry of access to personal information runs the risk of undermining those being monitored, making them feel they are being spied on. The issue of surveillance through digital technology will continue to have exposure and be debated across many sections of our society. How we engage with and shape public debate in this contentious area will determine the general acceptance and use of this technology and our own views of the society we inhabit in 2020 – and be a fruitful area for HCI researchers.

Questions for interaction and design
- How can monitoring technologies be designed to give feedback and control to those being observed, where it is considered desirable?
- Should people be able to opt out of being monitored and how do we design technology to do this?
- How can the capture of information and the need for privacy be balanced through design?

Questions of broader impact
- What ethical guidelines are needed for managing monitored information and how are these reviewed and implemented?
- Whose responsibility is it to ensure that systems for monitoring are designed to balance the rights of individuals with those of society?
- How do we ensure the monitoring of activities changes the behaviour of social groups and public behaviour for the better?

↑ CCTV cameras increasingly monitor behaviour in public places, leading many to fear for the growth of 'the surveillance society'.

2.6 The Growth of Creative Engagement

The new generation of technologies, including ubiquitous computing and Web 2.0, is enabling more creative uses of computing than ever before. Many of these are advancing our knowledge as a society. For example, various mixed-reality and sensor-rich physical environments have been developed to enable people to engage with both the physical and digital world in new ways. The most playful example of this is the Nintendo Wii. This is impacting on many aspects of learning, from science and medicine, to the way we teach our children through collaborative learning and experimental games. More extensive inquiries and decisions have been enabled, through the 'mash-up' of Web 2.0 tools, allowing for more discoveries and far-reaching analyses, such as determining the effects of deforestation in different continents.

More broadly, computers are now used for all kinds of creative engagement, and by all kinds of people. Whether for work or play, and whether they support research, hobbies, or home lives, technologies will enable us to take the initiative, be constructive, be creative and, ultimately, be in control of our interactions with the world. As we move toward 2020, we will have more flexibility in the tools we use and the content produced by them. And increasingly, we will use tools and content produced by all manner of people, from friends and family, to scientists and professionals.

Augmenting human reasoning

Computers are increasingly being used to visualise and reason about complex problems and information in new ways, leading to new forms of research. Computer scientists are working with biologists, chemists, physicists and earth scientists to develop computational tools that can help tackle some of the most important scientific questions facing the

In Vodafone's vision of the future, young musicians will be able to create music with friends in remote places, all following or creating a musical score together. A wraparound screen shows video images of friends and displays the digital score. →

world today, such as climate change and global pandemics. In its support of the doing of science, a challenge for the development of computational tools and technologies is to ensure that they are able to augment human reasoning and problem-solving skills in a way that empowers scientists' and others' ability to understand, model and solve problems.

We need to build tools that enable computing scientists and other scientists to share and communicate their expertise across disciplines. Building tools that can be used effectively across inter-disciplinary boundaries will require much more integration of the computing and other sciences than is currently the case. Not only that, but scientists in all disciplines are skilled professionals. Designing tools which are effective will depend on understanding the nature of their expertise. This raises all kinds of questions: are automated number-crunching tools that index, search and sort the way forward? Do we need other kinds of tools that model and highlight patterns, trends and anomalies in complex data and structures? To what extent do computer-based tools need to reveal and be explicit about their underlying assumptions and constraints? And as tools become more complex and work on ever greater datasets, it may be difficult to know when they malfunction, or when they are misapplied.

Another concern is how such tools represent complexity and make it tractable, whether it be modelling the earth's support systems or the human immune system. If a computer simulates a complex system, does it simply create a new one that needs further analysis and understanding? How can the ensuing knowledge be communicated and acted upon to solve problems in the world? For example, how can the results of computational analyses from many millions of data points be represented in meaningful ways? As we take on more complex problems, use more sophisticated models, and rely on increasingly powerful

computing resources and vast quantities of data, these issues will become more significant.

The ability to provide increasingly sophisticated tools to augment our human capabilities speaks strongly to the human values associated with our desire for productivity and industriousness in our lives, and our aspirations for greater knowledge. We will need to fathom out how best to represent and present information. This involves working out how to make data from all kinds of different sources intelligible, usable and useful. These may come from research labs, but equally may come from an ever-growing stream of data from the increasing array of sensors placed throughout the world. It also entails figuring out how to integrate and replay, in meaningful and powerful ways, the masses of digital recordings that are being gathered and archived, such that professionals and researchers can perform new forms of computation and problem-solving, leading to novel insights.

Questions for interaction and design
- Is further automation the way forward for augmenting human thinking and problem-solving?
- How can the interaction and design of new computational tools be structured so they do not impede creative engagement?
- What new toolkits can be developed to enable scientists, and others to create tools for themselves to solve their own problems and explore new avenues?

Questions of broader impact
- What will such tools mean for the nature of expertise in future?
- Will scientists become too dependent on tools? If so, what does this mean for the nature of invention and discovery?
- Will computer-based tools eventually become so complex they can no longer be understood by the people who developed them?

↑ **Microsoft's 'Surface' is an interactive tabletop allowing two-handed interaction with digital objects such as photos, music files, games and maps. These kinds of interactive surfaces encourage collaborative, creative engagement.**

New forms of creative engagement

Novel technologies, including interlinked tools, digital representations and physical artefacts, will offer the means to facilitate creative authoring, designing, learning, thinking and playing. They will allow different groups of people to participate in all kinds of new and engaging activities: from very young children to the elderly; from the amateur to the expert; and for many kinds of ability or disability. These toolkits will also offer up new opportunities in every aspect of life, and every part of the world. For example, educators and consultants are now able to use off-the-shelf toolkits to assemble and appropriate digital technologies to enhance learning for a range of settings, such as schools, waiting rooms, playgrounds, national parks, and museums. But even better, everyday users can now increasingly create their own content, grab content and applications off the Internet, and assemble their own digital resources just the way they want to.

How will we conceive of and design creative technologies? If we are now in the business of building tools rather than applications, and of providing digital resources rather than creating digital products, how does this change the nature of design? If people can assemble digital pieces to produce their own creations, this radically alters what it means to design an interface or a finished product. It may also mean changing design goals. Instead of designing usable products, it may mean we ought to worry more about designing flexible, versatile components. In addition, the role of good design changes when most of the designing is by the user. These are some of the new questions for interaction and design that are raised when users become their own producers, programmers and publishers.

Self-expression and the need for creativity are core human values. Many of us are driven to invent, appropriate and experiment. Powerful, flexible tools, whether they are everyday tools or sophisticated, state-of-the-art technology, allow us to express ourselves, pursue new ambitions and achieve new goals. For example, the ability to create and access new media through digital tools will allow us to augment our skills as artists and musicians, or support us in our personal hobbies, whether this be researching our family history, cooking, or trainspotting. But there are potential downsides and uncertainties as we move into the future. In a world where the design and development of new technologies become more decentralised, where new kinds of content and do-it-yourself applications become widespread and accessible to all, where will the control and the accountability be? Who will be responsible for making sure there is good design, and that the resulting technologies empower rather than undermine people? In a world where smarter and more flexible tools make us all experts, this raises the question of who will think about the larger societal and ethical impacts of what gets built.

Questions for interaction and design
- What is the role of interaction design when people exert more control over their digital resources and tools?
- What will the toolkits of 2020 be like if they are to encourage new and creative uses?
- Can tools be developed that encourage good design?

Questions of broader impact
- Who is accountable when amateurs build badly designed software?
- Who is responsible for having the 'bigger vision' of what technologies can do and should do?
- How will new forms of creative engagement change the role and ultimately the fate of the software developer, the designer and the usability engineer?

Summary

There are five main ways in which our interactions with computers will be transformed as we approach 2020. How we define and think about our relationships with computers is radically changing. How we use them and rely on them is also being transformed. At the same time, we are becoming hyper-connected and our actions, conversations and interactions are being increasingly etched into our digital landscapes. There is more scope than ever before to solve hard problems and allow new forms of engagement and creativity.

We have begun to raise the issues and concerns that these transformations provoke. There are many new kinds of questions we have not had to be concerned with before. Some will be within the remit of Human-Computer Interaction to address and others will not.

3 HCI: Looking Forward

Technology is changing, people are changing, and society is changing. All this is happening at a rapid and rather alarming rate. What can the HCI community do to intervene and help? How can it build on what it has achieved? In this Part we map out some fundamental changes that we suggest need to occur within the field. Specifically, we suggest that HCI needs to extend its methods and approaches so as to focus more clearly on human values. This will require a more sensitive view about the role, function and consequences of design, just as it will force HCI to be more inventive. HCI will need to form new partnerships with other disciplines, too, and for this to happen HCI practitioners will need to be sympathetic to the tools and techniques of other trades. Finally, HCI will need to re-examine and reflect on its basic terms and concepts. Outdated notions of the 'user', the 'computer' and 'interaction' are hardly sufficient to encompass all that HCI will need to attend to.

The Kiss Communicator is a concept prototype that allows you to blow a 'kiss' to your ➔ beloved even when in another part of the world. Squeezing and blowing on the device wirelessly sends a sequence of lights to its corresponding Communicator.

3.1 The Way Forward

Since its inception in the 1980s, HCI has been primarily concerned with designing more usable computer systems, be it the computer desktop, the VCR, the Web, or the mobile phone. It takes bad designs and shows how to improve them. And, it tries to apply its methods to design good systems from the start. But HCI needs to change what it does if it is to keep up with and influence the transformations in our midst.

By 2020, society's relationship with technology will be quite different from what it has meant to be 'users' of computers. Computers will quite literally be everywhere, from inside our bodies to roaming Mars. They will also look and feel quite different from the PCs, laptops or handheld computers of the 90s. There will be many opportunities to use them in diverse and novel ways not possible now, allowing us to express ourselves, be creative, and to nurture, protect, and care for one another in new ways. However, technological advances can equally support the darker side of what it means to be human. People may use them to find ever more sophisticated and subtle ways to control us, deceive us or spy on our every movement and transaction. Even if computers are not used with nefarious intentions, we could equally find ourselves in a world where we are bombarded with information, told what to do by our cars, offices and homes, forced to grapple with ever more complex technologies in our home and working lives, and monitored, measured and recorded without our knowing.

Do we simply let technological advances dictate what it will mean to be human in the age of ubiquitous computing or can HCI as an interdisciplinary community of researchers, practitioners and designers become more proactive in helping to shape society's new relationships with computer technologies?

A quite different mindset is needed for thinking about how to design for, how to control and how to interact with emerging ecosystems of technologies. While many researchers in HCI have begun to broaden their horizons, there is much work to be done. To begin, HCI needs to understand and analyse the wider set of issues that are now at play, most notably human values, including the moral and ethical aspects of designing technologies for new domains. The kinds of interactions we are designing for are beginning to have far-reaching consequences for people beyond the immediate actions they are engaged in. For example, designing a mobile communication device that makes visible to others in the vicinity a person's interests and dislikes may also enable anyone else in the street and beyond to permanently track, record and 'see' what that person is doing on their device. What we make visible and what we keep hidden at an interface, how that is accessed and how it is represented to others, will be affected by and affect, in turn, the social behaviours, norms, and practices that are considered ethical and acceptable.

So, how can the wider range of societal and moral concerns be addressed in interaction design? Moreover, is it possible to design a responsible army robot or an ethical data-capturing wallpaper? To broaden the remit of HCI, we propose a three-pronged approach that builds on its accomplishments. First, we suggest extending the way that user-centred research and design is conducted by including another stage of conceptual analysis that explicitly addresses these higher-level concerns, including the questions raised in Parts 2.2-2.6. A second way forward is to develop new partnerships with other disciplines that traditionally have not been part of HCI, but that are equipped to address societal, moral and ethical concerns. Third, we suggest redefining the basic building blocks of HCI, ie concepts of the 'human', the 'computer' and 'interaction'. A *lingua franca*, comprising new metaphors, concepts and principles, will enable the diverse parties to understand each other better, to talk about the emergent transformations, and to explore how to steer them in 'human' directions.

Central to the new agenda is recognising what it means to be human in a digital future. We suggest foremost that human values, in all their diversity, be better understood and charted in relation to how they are supported, augmented or constrained by technological developments. In many ways, we are arguing for a strengthening of what has always been important to HCI: a focus on human-centred design, keeping firmly in sight what users – people – need and want from technology. But beyond this, HCI needs to extend its approach to encompass how human desires, interests and aspirations can be realised and supported through technology. These have to be defined not just at the level of the individual, but also at the social, cultural and ethical level.

From User Experience to Human Values

As we have stressed throughout, computers, now more than ever, do much more than compute. When someone takes a digital photo and stores it on a PC, when they browse through their photo collections or post an image on a website for friends to see, they do not think of the computers that enabled them to do these things as undertaking computation. They think of the computers as letting them make, move and store 'stuff'. And if it is not about making and managing stuff, it might be about other things. It might be about playing games; it might be about creating personal noticeboards through websites; or it might be about

communicating with each other. In short, technologies do not necessarily 'solve problems' for users in the way they used to, say, 20-30 years ago, but increasingly are able to fulfil many other kinds of interests, desires or ambitions.

In recognition of the way computer use is changing, a number of researchers and practitioners have begun studying the nature of the 'user experience' and how it unfolds over time. This has largely involved defining its subjective qualities, such as what interacting with a device, like an MP3 player or a pet robot, feels like to use. Concepts such as pleasure, aesthetics, fun and flow, on the one hand, and boredom, annoyance and intrusiveness, on the other, have been used to describe the multifaceted nature of such 'felt' experiences. In addition, HCI specialists have modelled how we respond to technology from a visceral or emotional level through to a conscious, reflective one. They have also described the whole life-cycle of our response to technology, from when it first grabs our attention and entices us, through to our ongoing relationship with that technology. These alternative ways of conceptualising users' experience have opened many doors and new possibilities for design and research, especially for the way we understand individuals and individual experience.

In contrast, human values extend these notions about the individual to conceptions about what is desirable within a culture or a society. Values such as privacy, health, ownership, fair play and security are increasingly incorporated in the design of ubiquitous technologies. Members of society have their own views on which values they desire and treasure. Most often these values are not made explicit, but nonetheless they drive our behaviour both as individuals and as a society.

But making judgements about new computer technologies and how they will affect us is not straightforward. Computers may help us recollect the past; equally, it might be important for us to forget. They can help us be connected to others, but by the same token, it may be important that they allow us sometimes to be isolated. Likewise, computers can support our industriousness, but at other times, we may want to 'switch off' and be restful. Technologies can be designed specifically to support certain values, such as enabling people to express themselves, to demonstrate their affection to others, to nurture and to reassure family members. They can also be designed inadvertently to violate human values such as trust, privacy and a sense of fairness.

Taking into account the scope of human values, therefore, is quite a different undertaking than seeking to attain the design goals of efficiency, effectiveness and utility. Design trade-offs need to be considered not just in terms of time and errors, but in terms of the weighing up of the various moral, personal and social impacts on the various parties who will be affected by the proposed technology. For example, the design goal of a 'well being' monitoring technology for diabetic children might be to provide reassurance for parents that their child's blood sugar level is stable during school time when they are not around to assist. However, it is not only the parents that have to be considered but also the sensitivities of the child, the school nurse, the teachers and the other children. All are involved, to varying degrees. Hence, personal data should be represented and interacted with in a way that is not only usable but also socially acceptable. But it is not just the nature of the information and how it should be presented; how the device is to be worn by the child needs careful consideration. Ethical concerns arise as to whether the device should be designed so that the child is or is not able to remove it. And so on. The monitoring of others, the capture of, access to and management of people's personal information, however benign in its intentions, need to be understood within a social and moral context. It is no longer enough that we think about designing for users; we need also to think about how we design for families, communities and different social groups.

The values that we discover and decide to design for will vary from context to context. For example, the notion of privacy is very different in a family than it is in a workgroup. Knowing where your children are, and that they are safe and secure is part of the 'job' of being a parent. In a sense, it is part and parcel of home life. However, having access to the location and activities of your employees at work is a very different thing and may be viewed much more negatively. What is right and what is wrong is defined differently in different contexts.

How human values play out in relation to computing innovation will also become more critical as researchers come up with ever more ingenious and potentially intrusive ways of sensing, monitoring, collecting and sharing digital information. Importantly, we need to consider both the positive and negative aspects of the possibilities afforded by new technologies and software. For example, a recent innovation is turning mobile phones into swarming surveillance systems, through the development of software that uses BlueTooth to automatically collect and share information between phones and then collectively analyse the events that they record. On the positive side, such a technique may provide a good way of spotting wildlife in the savannah but, equally, it could be employed for more sinister activities, such as packs of school children using it to persecute and bully each other in more insidious ways.

It is important, too, to consider how the uptake of technologies is transforming our value systems. In our increasingly connected world, our notions of what it means to live on one's own, to be part of a family, to be a teenager, and to grow old are all changing as a result of how we use social networking tools, home entertainment systems, health monitoring systems, mobile communication technologies, and so on. An average teenager now has over sixty friends. But what does it mean to create, maintain and lose

'The bottom line is that computer technologies are not neutral – they are laden with human, cultural and social values'

friendships through digital technologies? How trustworthy are friendships made and maintained through websites? Is a teen with many online friends in fact more isolated than someone who has two close friends living next door? If we design ever more tools for communicating and staying in touch how will this affect the way we live?

The new technologies allow new forms of control or decentralisation, encouraging some forms of social interaction at the expense of others, and promoting certain values while dismissing alternatives. For instance, the iPod can be seen as a device for urban indifference, the mobile phone as promoting addiction to social contact, and the Web as subverting traditional forms of governmental and media authority. Neural networks, recognition algorithms and data-mining all have cultural implications that need to be understood in the wider context beyond their technical capabilities.

The bottom line is that computer technologies are not neutral – they are laden with human, cultural and social values. These can be anticipated and designed for, or can emerge and evolve through use and abuse. In a multicultural world, too, we have to acknowledge that there will often be conflicting value systems, where design in one part of the world becomes something quite different in another, and where the meaning and value of a technology are manifest in diverse ways. Future research needs to address a broader, richer concept of what it means to be human in the flux of the transformations taking place.

3.2 Extending the Research and Design Cycle

User-centred design and research typically follows an iterative cycle, comprising four fundamental processes in which we study, design, build and evaluate technology *(see figure on page 59)*. Different terms may be used, but fundamentally the four stages involve the same kinds of activities.

We propose that a new agenda for HCI should extend this design model, by adding one further stage, which entails conceptual analysis *(see figure on page 59)*. We label this stage 'understand'. While understanding a problem has traditionally been part of the study phase, we are proposing that it be elevated to become a more explicit process, where the various human values at play are thought through and the trade-offs examined in a systematic way. Philosophical debate, thought experiments and scenarios can form the basis of this process. Engaging in dialogues with professionals from other disciplines,

whose expertise lies in using such conceptual analytic methods, will be of considerable benefit. Involving a broader spectrum of designers (including architects and clothing designers) will also allow for different perspectives on human values to materialise.

Currently, the goal of a typical HCI research project is to design or re-design a particular computing technology (be it product, service, application, or system) in order to improve upon or enhance a given experience (eg shopping online) or to create a quite different experience than before (for example, constructing a novel ambient display for families).

In both situations, initial research is conducted by learning more about people's current experiences (such as using particular kinds of Web browsers to find out about houses for sale; sending text messages to one's children to check up on where they are if they are not where they said they would be at a given time). Ethnographic studies, logging of user interaction and surveys are commonly deployed. Based on the findings gathered, we begin to think about why, what, and how to design something better. To aid the process, usability and user experience goals are identified and conceptual models developed. Prototypes are built, evaluated, and iterated, demonstrating whether the user goals have been met or whether the new user experience is judged to be enjoyable, pleasurable or valuable by the target group.

The extended approach to HCI research and design is intended to enable human values to be folded into the mix at all of the various stages. While we refer to these various components as Stage 1 to Stage 5, we do not mean to imply they have a fixed starting point and must be followed in a strict sequence. The cycle, as is normally the case in HCI, can be entered into at any point, and usually iterates in the course of any research or design project.

Stage 1: Understand

The initial – and new – stage we suggest is to focus on human values and to pinpoint those that we wish to design for and to research. This will require reflective thought and conceptual analysis drawing on other disciplines, which might include those as diverse as philosophy, psychology, art, literary theory, cultural studies, anthropology, sociology or design. It will also mean talking to stakeholders, including users as well as those involved in developing or designing the technology in question (if this is the goal) to ascertain what kinds of enduring value they believe their users will get from their technology; and what kinds of users and what domains are of interest.

We might be interested in developing new digital tabletop applications, for example. This phase of work would involve clarifying what kinds of human values might be made possible through such interactions. Is it about supporting social connectivity and togetherness? Is it about play and creativity? Is it about archiving photographs and other materials to preserve and honour family history? Is it about allowing people to reminisce or reflect on their personal past? Or perhaps is it about supporting collaborative tasks in domestic situations?

Ultimately, this new stage of the cycle therefore results in making choices. It will also involve specifying what kinds of people are the focus of this particular project, and in what kinds of domains of activity, environments or cultures. In other words, it will involve choosing the kinds of value systems we are interested in. These investigations in turn will either point to some fundamental research which needs to be carried out in Stage 2, or will provide guidance toward relevant research which has already been carried out.

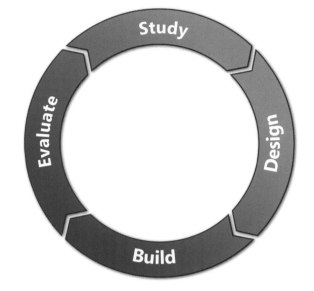

← The conventional user-centred, four-stage design/research model

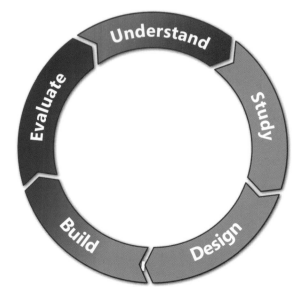

← Extended user-centred, five-stage design/research model. The new stage entails conceptual analysis or 'understanding'

Stage 2: Study

This stage of research consists of developing a deeper understanding of what factors are at play in how the values of interest are manifest in the everyday world. While Stage 1 provides a framework to guide design and research, this stage involves fleshing out the details of how individuals and social groups pursue and achieve those particular aspirations.

What is different about this kind of analysis compared with the canonical HCI approach is that, while a typical HCI project might only look at an individual's interaction or set of tasks or practices around a particular technology, the extended Study stage can be much broader. It begins by considering the details of particular tasks or practices, but then asks how those mechanics of interaction help people achieve long-lasting value through and beyond the interaction. Research might look at current shopping practices, for example, and focus on how they enforce social connections to other people, or help people acquire new objects to bolster their identity, or how the shopping experience provides distraction and disengagement from the world of work.

All of these are different higher-level values which are reflected in the specific behaviour of individuals, but are manifest, too, in the hopes and ideals of people, the way the environment is designed (technologically or otherwise), the social situation, and the cultural ideals of a place. This kind of analysis then does not just take into account people's interactions with computer technology, but looks at their interactions with the everyday world more broadly: in the environment, with everyday objects, with other people, as well with the hi-tech elements of their world. This is a more complex analysis, again involving input from disciplines outside of HCI, focusing on the forces that drive people to engage with technologies, and the ways in which those technologies are embedded in the world.

This stage usually entails conducting a user study of one sort or another. Often, this means ethnography, looking at particular kinds of people in particular contexts. Based on this, further user studies can be conducted to examine the ways in which specific kinds of behaviours interplay with specific values in a more controlled situation in the laboratory. For example, if the goal is to produce on-line shopping experiences that support trust between a shopper and an on-line process, this can be investigated in a focused study. It may also be the case, for a particular set of human values, that there is already a well-established body of work. The conceptual analysis from Stage 1 will help point to existing relevant work in this case, which may well include literature in other fields.

Hence, Stage 2 provides a grounded understanding of how the human values of interest are played out through interaction, taking into account social factors, environmental factors and so on. Essentially it provides a rich mix of perspectives and insights within which we can begin to imagine and sketch out different technological possibilities.

Stage 3: Design

The third stage is primarily a design or creative phase and involves reflecting on what the design goals should be. It could be that we want to engender, support, or amplify the human values in question. However, it could be that the design goal is to deepen our understanding of a set of values, a group of people, or a domain. In this case, we might want to design to provoke ambiguity in how a technology is used or interpreted, or even contradict the values we are interested in. These are techniques which have their roots more firmly in the world of art and design but which can be used to advance the research. Or it may be that we want to design for people to be designers; to provoke and inspire them into creative action. As such, our design goal may be harder to define, and the ultimate result of our own design work more difficult to foresee as we shift the point where the creativity really occurs in the development of a technological system.

The design phase needs to consider the culture and place in which the new technology will be situated, especially if they are such different social and physical ecosystems as schools, stations, churches, or civic squares. What will it mean to the different inhabitants? How might the technology be appropriated alongside other existing technologies and artefacts?

The emerging ecosystems of technologies will have far-reaching design implications for existing infrastructures, the people that inhabit those spaces, and the value systems already in place. For example, designing a smart phone needs to take into account not just the individual user experience of playing music, sending photos and receiving texts, but also how BlueTooth and other networking and sensing infrastructures will allow new forms of tracking, monitoring and public engagement. The potential for new hardware, software, and underlying infrastructures can equally inspire design. Sustainability of design is also an area with ramifications for human values we prioritise. It is all very well offering people new experiences, but at what cost?

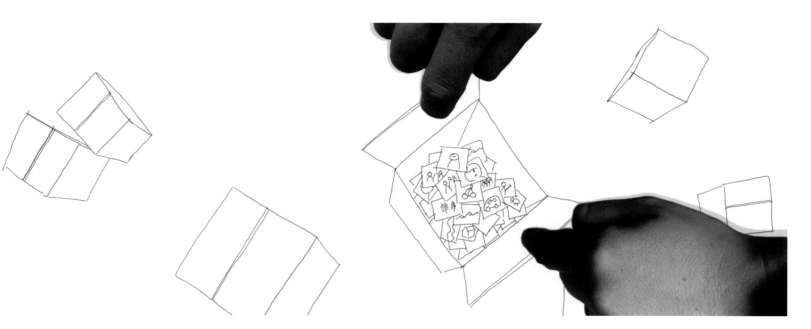

Stage 4: Build

This phase can involve anything from low-tech methods such as paper prototypes and sketches, to more hi-tech and robust systems ready for long-term field testing. Whereas, before, much of the building within HCI has been essentially software-based, entailing the development of, say, an interface for a desktop or a mobile device, as we move forward to 2020, what we build may be more hybrid. It may require both development of the software interface plus novel amalgams of hardware. For instance, cameras may be used as an input mode, rather than a keyboard. It might, as another example, involve the creation of everyday objects such as furniture, or parts of the built environment such as special walls or floors. It might even involve no interface at all in the traditional sense. For example, micro-payment devices simply require proximity and no interaction – touching, clicking or pointing – at all. Some interactions are distributed across different parts of a physical-digital ecosystem consisting of various devices and interconnecting sub-systems. Others have no interface in the sense that they are embedded within the everyday world and are not recognisable as computers. This does not mean that HCI research avoids building such systems. To the contrary, if these systems pertain to human values of some sort, then HCI must endeavour to explore and research them whatever their form.

The complexity of such hybrid systems might seem to imply that building them would be a slow, laborious process. It certainly would be if doing so required what one might call engineered quality. Instead, it will often mean building technologies which are sufficiently robust to test and explore the concept in question, and little more. If it turns out the concept appeals (according to whatever value is appropriate) then more polished engineering of the device or system will come later.

Fortunately, there are various tools and technologies now that allow researchers to undertake many kinds of building tasks quickly and easily.

Physical toolkits (eg 'phidgets' – see left), can be used to rapidly assemble complex amalgams of software and hardware using Lego-like building blocks consisting of various sensors and controllers.

Each element performs one or two tasks and can be easily programmed to interconnect with other elements and other computers. Thus, experiences as diverse as interaction between a wearable device communicating to a situated device – a wearable camera might send its images to be displayed on a nearby screen – or a novel set of handheld devices that allow gesture-based mode of input and output, can be built without the need for expensive machine-tooling or advanced programming.

There are other tools and technologies on the market which offer similar opportunities for lightweight prototyping. Of course this does not mean that the building stage in any particular programme of research will always be easy and quick; clearly it will depend upon the goal. Besides, HCI researchers will continue to use older techniques for building too, such as virtual simulations and even *Wizard of Oz* techniques when it becomes wholly impractical to build an entirely functional system. In this approach, some function of the system can be performed by a human who is invisible to the user (like the said wizard).

Whatever the technique or the technology used in this stage, the goal is to build something, in whatever fashion, that allows researchers to produce evidence about the experience they are trying to enable. Only then can researchers turn to the next stage, evaluation.

↑ **Phidgets or 'physical widgets' are building blocks to help developers construct physical user interfaces. These arose from a research project led by Saul Greenberg at the University of Calgary.**

Stage 5: Evaluate

The fifth stage involves evaluation of what has been built. Design work can only ever represent a best guess at what kind of solution will achieve some research and design goals. This is the stage at which that best guess is tested. Here, existing HCI methodologies can be used. There are many techniques to draw on: from focus groups to laboratory evaluations to *in situ* field tests of technologies and so on. Guidance as to what kind of evaluation technique is appropriate comes, in part, from the design or research goal, of course. When values become part of the research agenda, though, what counts as pertinent and relevant to evaluation is also altered and broadened. If the values are related to, say, digital footprints, then evaluation might concern itself with whether a chosen design delivers useful resources for, let us say, government monitoring or, by way of contrast, for an individual amassing personal data. What counts as good and bad, as worthwhile or invasive, will vary accordingly. In other words, the set of criteria against which a design is to be evaluated will be closely bound to the type of values being pursued.

At the same time, when evaluation occurs, it is almost certain that the delivery of one value will have implications for other values that may be in one way or another dependent upon it. Moreover, delivering one value may contradict another value in ways that had not been expected prior to the evaluation. In other cases, they may have unexpected benefits over and above the original intentions. For example, aspects of digital footprints that are designed to satisfy the desires of an individual may have knock-on benefits or drawbacks for governments.

A further challenge in evaluation for HCI in 2020 will be the need to assess some of the longer term and more far-reaching impacts of the design in question, and again this

'The delivery of one value will have implications for other values'

might point towards values that seem somewhat distant from the one originally designed for. A concern for these values in the evaluation stage is necessary, though, since it will enable researchers to provide more extensive accounts of how the devices and services operate in a wider context.

Any of these various considerations might make HCI researchers revisit their original design. For this reason, the iterative process remains important. Nevertheless, these considerations may also suggest to HCI researchers that other experts from other disciplines need to participate in evaluation. A further goal of this stage might be then for HCI researchers to identify what expertise outside of their domain may be required.

← A new device being evaluated in a long-term field trial in a family kitchen.

63

3.3 Three Case Studies

To illustrate how HCI research can embrace human values throughout the various phases and to show the benefits of doing so, three case studies are presented here. Each explores both the positive and negative possibilities that the technology of concern can engender. They also cover areas that are topical and contentious: trading versus trafficking content, tracking versus surveillance in families, and finally, exploring the set of values involved in augmenting human memory.

Case Study 1: Trading versus trafficking content

Overview: an investigation of the design of services and applications for mobile TV is a case study of how one might use the extended HCI approach. A concern for values in addition to a concern for usability led to a new direction for the design of mobile TV services and applications. The study also highlights the need to make choices about certain values and the price that sometimes comes with such choices. Differences in the weight one gives to different values can have a profound impact on system design, right the way down to the design of its operating system. [See Bibliography: Harper, Regan et al, 2007]

This research needs to be placed in context. It was undertaken at a time where two trends appeared to be merging, creating opportunities for new kinds of interactions. On the one hand, there was the convergence of different content 'channels' allowing many different types of content (such as radio, voice, and broadcast TV) to be delivered on many kinds of device. On the other, there was a trend (continuing today, obviously) toward the miniaturisation of technology. This allowed the consumption of content originally designed for larger devices to be achieved on progressively smaller ones. Inevitably, this trend was leading to the emergence of mobile phones that afforded 'TV watching'.

For traditional HCI, where the model of the human is essentially an information-processing one, the task for research in relation to this convergence is easy to define. First, it would seek to investigate such things as the minimal required level of visual or auditory quality to enable a user to have a good experience watching that content on a small device. Second, it would be to explore how the design of the devices in question should allow the user to engage in that experience easily and efficiently.

As it happens, these two concerns have been the topic of a great deal of HCI research. There is a considerable body of work on mobile TV that treats the subject as one of compatibility between the human eye and the constraints of a hand-held TV display device, for example. This literature is predominantly based on laboratory studies of different screen resolutions and compression algorithms. There is also a great deal of work concerned with the design of electronic programme guides (or EPGs – *Radio Times* as big as a credit card) and making these easy and efficient to use. These of course must be designed somewhat differently to those offered on normal TV screens because of size constraints.

One particular concern reported in this research is that some compression algorithms systematically remove small objects from mobile TV on the grounds that they are 'noise'. This is rather irksome when the users in question are trying to watch football (or ice hockey) on their mobile phones. This aside, the gist of this general 'speeds and feeds' research is that there is a need to be better on all fronts: compression algorithms need to compress more effectively, and EPGs need to be easier to use (demanding fewer clicks per selection, for example).

Yet we would claim that such research, though necessary, only points to some of the basic requirements that HCI should attend to. It does not sufficiently encompass all the values related to the use of mobile TV, nor does it explore whether there might be contradictions in the types of values that might be enabled through mobile TV. Another way of putting this is that the existing body of research does not begin by ascertaining which human values might be pertinent to the mobile TV experience. Rather, the bulk of it deals with what one might call the 'usability problem' of allowing users to view TV anywhere, anytime.

A different approach could begin with an investigation of the values at play in viewing mobile TV, one that begins with Stage 1, a conceptual analysis of the problem. Such an analysis seeks to determine the range of purposes, goals, intentions, and motives – in a phrase, the possible set of values that lead users to use mobile TV. Crucial to this stage is recognition, at the outset, that the consumption of mobile TV may not be the same as the consumption of TV in normal settings. It recognises that other values might be relevant, and that the idea of 'anytime, anywhere' TV watching may not be particularly pertinent to the types of experiences that people seek.

In fact there are glimmerings of this within the existing body of HCI research in this area. Some studies report that users are remarkably tolerant of the experience afforded by mobile TV devices. It turns out that they are happy to watch mobile TV, whatever the screen resolution, even watching football when they can't see the ball. All they really desire, apparently, is to claim to have 'seen the goal'. Another finding in this literature is that in trials (if not in laboratory studies), the primary value of TV content on the phone would not appear to be to watch TV, as if mobile TV was a substitute for more traditional TV watching practices. Rather, users seem to delight in using broadcast content on mobiles to augment their real experiences, such as replaying a goal right after it

'Users seem to delight in using broadcast content on mobiles to augment their real experiences'

occurred while at a football match. And here it is not just about reliving the moment. Rather, in doing so they are also sharing that experience with the people they are with. So, for example, fans of one side of the football match might keep replaying the goal their side had scored to torment their friends who are fans of the opposing side.

In short, conceptual analysis leads to the recognition that 'TV-in-the-hand' may support other things that a person might be doing, apart from literally holding a TV in the hand. It may support a person's ability to claim that they watched something 'for real' for instance, or to share a moment again and again with a friend nearby. Mobile TV might not primarily be about consumption of multimedia content by an individual, then, but be more about the social use of that material. This means the substitution of traditional TV might not be the important issue. Rather, it might be how mobile TV augments social connectivity. The values pertaining to this might be quite different from the values in relation to 'anytime, anywhere' media consumption. These suggestions attest to the need to properly reflect and conceptually locate the kinds of human endeavours we are thinking of for these devices.

This leads onto Stage 2, which is essentially empirical and concerns itself with how the values in question are played out in everyday life and might also lead to the recognition of other related values. As it happens, in this case, there are studies of related activities. There are, for instance, many ethnographies of how cameraphones are creating

65

opportunities for people to enrich their experiences. These studies show that instead of photos being *of* an event, they become *part of* that event. This is bound up with the disposability and ephemeral nature of digital imaging. People take lots of images with their phones because it costs nothing and because doing so makes experiences more fun.

Other studies show that, just as capturing images can enhance the moment, so mobile phones are being used as a new means of sustaining, embodying and creating social networks. The literature here is replete with studies showing how people exchange phone numbers, images, and text messages, both when they are together and when they are apart. They do so as a means of creating solidarity. What mobile phones allow for is the creation and sharing of new 'digital currencies' that bring people together.

Reading the empirical literature of course is only part of what might be necessary in Stage 2. Sometimes first-hand studies might be required too. In this case, the researchers (a team from a mobile operating system company and a content provider) were able to examine and interview users about the kinds of mobile multimedia they downloaded and watched. They found confirmation that these users were augmenting their real-time experiences, as was suggested by the mobile TV literature. But the research also found that they were engaged in the routine exchange of files, via BlueTooth, to create similar processes of social bonding that the literature suggests is achieved with SMS and other messaging forms. The researchers found that, beyond this, the exchanging of multimedia files has come to have various social codes associated with it, such as the need for the receiving of a file to be reciprocated by the giving of one, the consequence of which is that there is a kind of 'economic' system at work, albeit without money.

The researchers came to call the system of exchange they had uncovered 'trafficking'. The term was chosen for more than simply the trading allusion, however. For the researchers found that the users in question were concerned that the exchange of such materials might infringe digital rights; they were also aware that some of the materials exchanged could be viewed by some people as offensive, even pernicious. This was trafficking then because it was a kind of illicit behaviour and one that might not be 'good' for the user. This highlights the potential negative side of the values achieved in these behaviours.

The point here is that sensitivity to the values in question was developed through the application of conceptual analysis as well as an empirical study (Stages 1 and 2). With this as a basis, Stage 3, design, was the next step.

In this case, the designs that were proposed entailed treating mobile TV not as a way of creating a substitute for traditional TV watching, but as a means for enabling a different set of values to be supported, namely, techniques for allowing people to enrich their real experiences and to create bonds between themselves. More specifically, what was designed was a system whereby users could download segments watched on conventional TVs onto their mobile devices. The goal here was to allow the user to augment their experience by letting them watch a chosen moment again and again. Football goals came to mind, as did funny moments in sitcoms and so forth. Second, and as a key part of this design, the system was also built to allow the downloaded files to be exchanged with other mobile users.

In Stage 4, the system was built, the technology chosen for exchange relying on BlueTooth. The resulting prototype enabled users to collect or 'grab' content, and then trade or 'traffick' it later on. The prototype system meant that trafficking was richer than what had been possible before, since it could include TV segments downloaded to the mobile as the user watched traditional TV.

This system was then evaluated, as part of an overall iterative design process, constituting Stage 5. It is worth discussing this evaluation process as it highlights how a concern for human values can be of great consequence, even down to the basic assumptions of the design of an operation system.

In the evaluation of the trafficking system, participants in a trial readily understood the concept of downloading segments from their TVs, and were able to grab content quite easily. A problem emerged, however, when they tried to exchange or 'traffick' files with other people.

This can be illustrated with the experience of one individual. This person found downloading straightforward and could select a file to exchange. He had no problem discovering a nearby BlueTooth device either and could send to that device. However, he then went on to say, even before he had attempted to exchange a file, that he knew it wouldn't work. He showed the research team this was true by demonstrating how he could find a

discoverable BlueTooth device, choose a file and send it. He then drew attention to how the receiving device would show an 'accept file' dialogue box as if a file transfer was happening. He then pointed out that once that dialogue box disappeared, the device went back to its idle state. 'Nothing happens,' he exclaimed. 'It doesn't work!'

The researchers were perplexed by this since they knew that the files had in fact been transferred. What had occurred was a consequence of the design of the particular mobile phone used in the trial. This device, based on the Windows Mobile operating system, places, by default, all files sent by BlueTooth into the 'My Documents' folder under the 'Explorer file directory manager'. Further, such files are listed, alphabetically, under their own name. There are good reasons for this design. Developers of Windows Mobile assume that users want their mobiles to act in the same way as their personal computers, filing things neatly away in a hierarchical system. The assumption is that this efficiency and consistency is what mobile users will value.

However, the consequence of this design is that when a file exchange occurs, the exchanged file seems to disappear, the phone instead defaulting to what one might call the

The left hand image shows the states that the Windows Mobile device goes through, first showing the file in the process of being received and second, once the file has been received.
The right hand image shows the same states on a Symbian device. It is the end point of both experiences that is at issue: one indicates nothing about the presence of a new file (it being tidily placed in the My Documents folder); the other draws attention to it, presenting it in the Inbox. ←

'Design for values can and often will lead to profound choices'

'desktop'. To find the file in question, users have to open up Explorer and click through to the 'My Documents' folder. Despite all the users being familiar with this occurring on their personal computers, all of the users in this study found this at odds with their expectations in this different kind of situation.

It turned out that their expectations were more consistent with mobile phones that run a different operating system such as Symbian. On these devices, when files are sent via BlueTooth, the operating system treats any file like a message, regardless of what type it is. This means an SMS message and a multimedia file sent by BlueTooth are both presented to the user in the same way once the transfer has occurred, namely by appearing in the 'Inbox'. The result of this is that when a BlueTooth file transfer has completed, the user is presented with a dialogue box that prompts them to click through to the new message *(these differences are highlighted in the figures on page 67).*

Recognising this difference was something of an epiphany for the research team. It was only at that point that they realised that the design of their mobile devices, though perhaps ideal for other practices, did not fit practices oriented towards trafficking. They came to recognise that the important difference between Symbian and Windows Mobile devices was not in terms of number of clicks or menus, but rather had to do with how the interface supported the values in question. With one, the recipient of a file felt as if they had a virtual object 'in the hand'. With the other, it was as if something had been exchanged, but that the computer (in the device) had consumed it.

Beyond this issue, the research also highlighted the other sets of values being played out when trafficking was undertaken. The most obvious had to do with digital rights. The production and the broadcasting of TV content obviously costs money. The design of the system does not deal with that problem. It allows users to grab any piece of TV content without a payment system. In a sense, it allows users to thieve.

But the issue was not quite as simple as that either. The content provider in question viewed the ability of users to download and traffic segments of their content as an opportunity to foster 'viral marketing'. All that was important from their perspective was that their brand be conveyed at the point of transfer. In this way, the person trafficking was, in effect, paying by supporting this advertising. Whether the user would be happy doing this was a question that the research did not address. The lesson here is that enabling one set of values might lead to implications for another set. Design for values is not always straightforward.

Finally, another concern had to do with the choice of content for trafficking. The design assumes that users want to grab TV content to trade. But it also allows users to trade in other files, gathered from other places. And while broadcast TV content is editorialised and subject to agreed levels of taste and propriety, other kinds of files may not be. Indeed, some kinds of content might be self-created precisely because they are intended to be offensive. Or such materials might be downloaded from the largely unregulated world of the Web. This means that supporting trafficking might end up encouraging the exchange of files to support values other than social cohesion or in-the-moment laughter and fun. Rather, it could support exploitation and dubious behaviour of various kinds and even criminality instead. Again the moral here is that design for values can and often will lead to profound choices. Moreover it also serves to remind us that the links between values are not always clear or distinct.

Case study 2: Tracking versus surveillance in families

Overview: This study looks at the home and considers new kinds of technologies that could be used to enrich family life. In particular, in the past few years there has been a range of technologies developed that use wireless networking and location information to help families keep track of each other. There are numerous services to subscribe to that let parents track their children via their mobile phones; GPS devices that can be worn as a wristwatch or sewn into a jacket letting parents view children on satelllite maps; and even chips that can be inserted under a child's skin much as one might micro-chip a pet. [See Bibliography: Brown et al, 2007; Taylor et al, 2007]

With tracking technologies, a range of human values come into play. On the one hand, they raise the ire of civil libertarians and conjure up the spectre of Big Brother: we are using technology more and more to watch people's every move. This is one step further toward a total surveillance society. Moreover, monitoring of this sort (within the parent-child relationship) is asymmetric: power and control lie with one party and not the other. The flip side of this is that it is all about giving children more freedom and independence. If parents are able to worry less about where their children are, they are more likely to allow them their autonomy. Tracking, they argue, is about caring, not intruding.

Against the backdrop of the ongoing debates, and as the result of some earlier work investigating how families communicate, the research project team in this case became convinced that awareness was a key value for families which technology might be able to support. Here they had in mind the importance of awareness in supporting the management of what can often be complex, day-to-day activities. The goal then was primarily to build a device which would allow families to more effectively plan activities, organise themselves and to communicate better with each other. But they also realised that developing a system

to support families with location-based information needed to start with a conceptual analysis (ie Stage 1). In this case, they reflected on both the positive and negative aspects of what it means to monitor and keep track of the people one cares about. These included more positive values such as facilitating the coordination of activities in social groups, as well as more negative ones such as intrusion into personal privacy. And it also included considering the various factors that might determine the trade-offs involved. This entailed questions such as: At what point does monitoring become spying? What is it about the nature of the relationship between the person monitoring and the person being monitored which makes the difference? What are the contextual issues that might influence this?

With regard to contextual issues, the researchers considered the ways in which values from tracking systems might be quite different in different kinds of social groups, different places and even different cultures. Here, the decision was to design a device for families with children. There is a large literature not just in HCI but in sociology, anthropology, cultural studies and the like that the researchers drew on to deepen their understanding of how these kinds of technologies might play out in families. The literature suggested that the way location-based information is used in the home might be quite different from the way it is used in other situations, such as at work. However, in advance, it was difficult to know just what the value for families would be.

Stage 2 of the research therefore involved grounding this analysis in more detailed studies of home life. As it turns out, the project team was able to make use of the growing body of work in HCI evaluating location-based systems for tracking friends and work colleagues. As another activity, they studied a handful of families in-depth to look at their current practices with regard to how they maintained awareness of each other's day-to-day activities using ordinary technologies such as mobile phones and notes, but more generally understanding how different members of those families were accountable to one another.

'Values such as reassurance, togetherness and enchantment call for different ways of thinking about how we design technology'

This then led to Stage 3 where the team began to sketch out the design of a device that they hoped would support awareness for families, without the more negative connotations of spying or surveillance. The result was a device they called 'The Whereabouts Clock' – a kitchen display designed to show the general whereabouts of family members, using the location of their mobile phones. The research team wanted the Clock to allow people at home to see at a glance where everyone in the family was at any point in time. When Dad leaves work, or the kids are on their way home from school, the Clock chimes as they move from one segment of the Clock to another, letting people at home know of their imminent arrival.

In designing the Clock, there were several key features the researchers thought might support the positive aspects of awareness without infringing on people's privacy. First, they designed the device to be situated within the family home and viewable only in the home. This meant that the right to see information on the Clock was tied to a person's entitlement to be physically in the home. Second, they designed the Clock so it showed only coarse-grained information about any person's whereabouts. When family members are out and about, information from their cell phone places them in the 'home', 'school', or 'work' regions of the clock (or in a region which means 'elsewhere'). These categories can be contrasted with the more accurate and fine-grained information that GPS and other location-based information can broadcast. Accuracy of information is often seen as a feature of the commercially-based systems. Here, the designers wanted to give as little information about location as possible. Third, they wanted the Clock to

show everyone in the family together rather than focusing only on children or on one person at a time. The fact that everyone is then given equal status on the display they thought would symbolise the fact that everyone is equally accountable, and would emphasise the family as a unit. A final design decision was that it was important to offer this information 'at a glance': that is, without requiring time to turn the device on, or change the status to view its settings.

Stage 4 involved building a number of prototypes and a robust infrastructure to enable researchers to conduct studies of the Clock's use in people's actual homes. The aim was to enable a real-world study to be conducted to assess how human values play out in practice over a long period of time. The result was a robust prototype that looked like a clock both in the design of its physical shape and its interface (see illustration, right).

In Stage 5, the Clock was deployed in five family homes and studied over a period of six months. Here the research team was both surprised by the positive way in which families incorporated the device into their everyday lives, but also by the value that the Clock turned out actually to deliver. While the Clock was originally designed with the goal of supporting activity management and planning for busy families, what they found was that the Clock was valuable not because it communicated what families didn't know about their loved ones' whereabouts, but rather because it confirmed what they already knew. In other words, the Clock was mainly valued because it let the family know 'all is right with the world', and that everyone was where they were supposed to be. The Clock therefore mainly supported reassurance rather than task management. It let families show that they cared for each other and were accountable to each other.

Moreover, the Clock was also valued because it became a symbol of the togetherness of the family. It not only made families feel more connected to each other, but showing all members of the family's icons together reinforced each person's notion of what it meant to be a family. It supported and displayed their identity as a family unit. One example here was a household with grown-up children who had recently moved into their own homes. Here, the parents liked to see that their children were nestling at 'home' even though home was not the same physical place it had been, or indeed one that they all shared. This result highlights how home is as much an ideal or a concept as it is a place.

Finally, the Clock was discussed as having almost magical properties. Something about the aesthetics of its design and the way people moved around the screen, sometimes chiming into 'home' before they walked in the door created a sense of wonder about the device which families were drawn to.

One conclusion to draw from this is that the decision to focus on one set of values, namely supporting awareness and coordination in family homes, ended up in fact supporting a range of other important, and in some ways unanticipated values. Reassurance and feeling connected were key here, as was the ability to show to others in the family that they cared for and were accountable to each other. These values in fact turned out to be much stronger and, in terms of this technology at least,

were more important than supporting 'getting things done'. This set of revelations made the team re-examine their earlier assumptions and gave them a new understanding of what they might design for in the future.

Another important point is that values such as reassurance, togetherness and enchantment call for different ways of thinking about how we design and evaluate technology. For example, because the Clock was not primarily a communication device, there was no need for a high degree of resolution of the information displayed – family members had no need to know exactly where someone else was. The rather coarse-grained way information was shown was, for the purposes of these families, 'good enough'. Further, they also expressed no concerns about privacy, which confirmed that in this respect the research team's design decisions had succeeded. But more than this, the researchers learned that it is part and parcel of family life to know what others in their family are up to and to share that information. The success of this device, therefore, had little to do with what we might understand to be work-oriented criteria about such things as accuracy of information, protection of information and so on. Rather, it shows that we need to design as much for our ideas and aspirations in life as we do the task in hand.

← The Whereabouts Clock: the lefthand image shows the clock in its case; the middle image is a close-up of its interface; and the righthand image shows what happens when you touch on a text message.

Case study 3: The 'value' of augmenting human memory

Overview: this study considers the human values associated with a research topic more generally; namely, how to design new technologies that can augment human memory. Memory is fundamental to what it means to be human not only in the way it defines who we are and bolsters our identity, but in how it helps us function in everyday life. At the same time, memory is notoriously fallible. As a result, the human tendency to forget is often invoked as the motivation behind a recent surge in technical efforts to build technology to provide all-encompassing support for human memory. So-called 'life-logging' systems, for example, aim to save every bit of information we ever touch, record every event we experience, and log every action we take. These systems aim, in other words, to create ever larger and more comprehensive personal archives of data (eg pictures, sounds, documents, location data), or what we have called earlier, digital footprints.

Lifelogging, it is proposed, will change forever how we use and share personal data, enabling us to look back over our lives and search through past experiences. New technologies, in sum, will give us all a comprehensive set of 'digital memories' to augment, or even replace, our biological ones. [See Bibliography: Harper, Randall et al, 2007; Harper, Randall et al, 2008; Sellen et al, 2007]

But just what benefits will these efforts bring us? Will these technologies really help us to know ourselves better, make our lives richer, strengthen our connections to those we care about and bring us closer to the world around us? And what are the appropriate research questions here? How do we design these potentially complex and far-reaching technological systems? As we embrace the emergence of digital footprints in the bigger sense we have described, where this footprint has all sorts of properties, content and possible uses, just what we mean by memory and, further, what aspect of memory we might be interested in designing for, need careful consideration by HCI researchers.

To tackle these new kinds of questions, Stage 1 begins by taking a step back from the initial assumptions which appear to be driving this class of technology and asks what we mean by human memory, and how this relates to fundamental human values. What aspects of memory will make our lives richer? In what situations might we want to remember and why? And even, is it sometimes better and more desirable to forget?

None of these questions makes much sense, however, until we first establish what long-term values we wish to support. As suggested earlier, this process is helped along by appealing to other perspectives and disciplines on these different topics, such as considering what cognitive psychology has to say about memory, or what are the views of philosophers and sociologists.

Next, we can begin to discern many kinds of human values that the concept of memory is linked to. For example, memory might be about supporting productivity and efficiency in one's working and personal life. This would imply developing tools that help us retrieve information we may need as easily and as accurately as possible (such as people's names, documents we may have lost, dates when important events occurred and so on). If that is the case, the technology need not help people truly relive or re-experience events from their past, only access the information they are after. It might also focus on memory not for past events but – paradoxically – for the future, in the sense of providing triggers to help people remember their intentions, remind them of their appointments and so on.

On the other hand, it may be that the purpose of the personal archive or digital footprint is to promote a person's individual sense of identity. In this case, helping people re-experience or truly recollect events from their personal past is much more important. The value here is through evoking that connection with autobiographical events and experiences, and says that we ought to be thinking about the kinds of materials that would trigger such recollections.

However, it might be that the main motivation for this class of technologies is more about the sharing of the past with others; it might really be about strengthening our connections to others we care about by providing materials that help us tell stories about them. In this sense, the technology we are designing and the research questions we would have in mind would be directed more toward issues of interpersonal entertainment, of theatre, and of 'in-the-moment' sharing with others. Memory in this sense is not so much about the past as it is about how the past is enacted in the present.

'In what situations might we want to remember and why? And is it sometimes better and more desirable to forget?'

There are many other human values that might also be looked at here, including the collection of personal data for the purpose of reflection on the patterns in one's life; or it might be about honouring and connecting the family to a shared past; and many more besides. The point here is that 'memory' means many things when analysed as a multi-faceted concept. And the value of a class of technologies which supports memory is rich and diverse. An initial step is to disentangle what that set of values might be, and to choose which are of most interest. It is therefore at this point largely a conceptual analysis.

Stage 2 moves on from the conceptual unpacking of Stage 1 to ask how the human values of interest are played out in everyday life. This stage may involve fieldwork; actually going out and looking at what currently goes on in everyday life. It would also involve taking into account existing literature, not just in HCI but in other relevant fields too.

Deciding what is of relevance here is determined by the human values of interest. Not surprisingly, different kinds of values point toward examining different kinds of cultural and social contexts, encompassing different practices and artefacts in people's lives. So for example, if the goal is to support people in more productive and efficient lives, this would point to the large body of work on personal information management practices in offices, the way people use reminders, the ways in which people do focused search for well-defined facts and so on. There is already a large literature in HCI which tells us about the kinds of memory problems people have at work, and offers insights into the way it might be usefully presented.

73

'Different human values guide us in different directions, both in terms of the literature we need to look at, and the work that needs to be carried out'

If it is about recollection and reliving one's personal past, there are different issues at stake and a different literature to turn to. Here there is a large amount of research in autobiographical memory in psychology. However, much of that work makes little connection to the kinds of materials one might capture with digital lifelogging technology (such as images, ambient sound, location and so on). This suggests that some experimental work needs to be done to understand the relationship between the kinds of cues one can capture, and the way in which it might trigger recollection for people.

Likewise, if the topic of interest is about storytelling with others, there is some work to turn to in HCI looking at how people engage in 'photo talk' around printed photographs in home settings. One might start also by looking at both the written word and the spoken word in sociological and anthropological research; and even at the design of theatre and broadcast content. The point is that, again, different human values guide us in different directions, both in terms of the literature we need to look at, and in terms of the field or experimental work that needs to be carried out.

Once the conceptual landscape has been mapped out, and the empirical details and insights gathered, the next stage, Stage 3, is to determine the design goals, and then to imagine what assembly of different technologies, applications and devices might help achieve those goals.

For example, the goal might be to design systems that can help elderly people with memory problems re-establish their sense of identity with others, and to help them socially engage with those they care about. In other words, the data from digital footprints might be used quite differently as materials for storytelling with others about aspects of the past that people can talk about with authority. We might, for example, begin to think of ways that elderly, housebound people can 'play back' materials to share with others. Here, the design process would benefit from input from clinical psychologists, product designers who specialise in the home, and perhaps even people with a film background to think about how the materials might be best edited and presented. The social milieu of the home and relationships to carers and family all need to be considered as input to the design, as do technical constraints and possibilities.

It is important to recognise that many possibilities might be pursued. The myriad roles that memory has in everyday life suggest one might imagine many different sorts of social technical landscapes. HCI can be involved in devising technologies that support a productive life; that support the art of conversation; that support personal identity and connection to our past; or even support forgetting. A focus on human values will provide important guidance but at the same time will open up a rich space of possibilities. These values will also help us make decisions about bigger issues to do with the design of interaction, such as questions of effective data management, who should have ownership of personal data, and how people's privacy can be protected. These decisions of course are fundamental to pointing us toward certain designs and not others, and in determining what we build in Stage 4.

Stage 5 is the point at which designs, prototypes, or probes are subject to evaluation, field deployment, focus group testing and other kinds of methodologies. Office memory-support systems might be tested in real workplaces; systems to support recollection might be evaluated in a more controlled setting to test the power of the materials in sparking recall; different designs for a 'storytelling' device might be presented to groups of older people for feedback and more informal evaluation.

But of course with all such technological developments, there are much more consequential issues that could be raised. To what extent do we want our everyday lives to be dependent on memory-support systems? What happens when these systems go wrong? If we collect and amass data about people who may be handicapped or elderly, how much should be done without their awareness? Who owns their data when they are gone? If we build life-logging systems for one group of people with their consent, how do we protect the rights of people whose movements and activities might as a by-product be captured by those same technologies? Can they opt out? How should society manage the storage and access of human data ethically and responsibly? How can the privacy and security of digital footprints be ensured to prevent misuse but at the same time allow them to be shared with others when needed? How do people find out about their digital footprint and what tools should be provided?

← The Digital Shoebox, by designer Richard Banks of Microsoft Research Cambridge UK, is an attempt to make the storage of digital photos more tangible. Photos can be sent wirelessly to the box, and users can browse through them by running their finger across the top of the box.

3.4 New concepts, frameworks and theories

The final proposition for a new agenda for HCI is that we need new concepts, frameworks and theories. In other words, in order to broaden HCI, we need a new *lingua franca* to enable us to talk to one another, especially when it comes to exploring the nuances of human values in the context of design and change.

It should include new ways of conceiving of the 'human' in HCI or the 'users', especially given that people are nowadays as much consumers, creators and players as they are users of computers. Conceptualising the emotional and pleasurable aspects of experiencing technologies is already starting to happen. Terms like 'magic', 'enchantment', 'fun', 'wonder', 'excitement' and 'surprise' have begun to creep into our vocabulary when thinking about the value of technology to people. But we need to ask what do these terms really mean and how do technologies engender these experiences? The aesthetics of computational products has also gained importance in terms of understanding better user satisfaction and reflection. Again, new models and frameworks would provide a better understanding of how these aspects of the user experience relate to human values.

At the same time, we need to have a new conception of the 'computer' in HCI. We need a better way of understanding how the embedding of digital technologies in everyday artefacts, in the built structures around us and in the natural landscape is transforming our surrounding environment into a physical-digital ecosystem. We now need to address not just the design of the artefacts themselves but also the spaces within which these artefacts reside. More than this, design has to deal with deeper, systemic issues. As the computer becomes more reliant on a larger world, and in particular as the connection to a network becomes essential, the opportunity for improving the user experience simply through a better interface is rapidly disappearing. We need concepts, frameworks and methods that will enable us to consider people and computers as part of a messy world full of social, physical, technical and physiological limitations and opportunities.

It follows that the 'I' in HCI – interaction – will need to be understood at many different levels too. First, it will be necessary to think about different 'sites of interaction', for example interactions on and in the body; between bodies; between bodies and objects; and at the scale of kiosks, rooms, buildings, streets and public spaces. All of these different levels of interaction offer different physical and social parameters that technologies can potentially change.

In a world in which people's movements and data transactions can be tracked and where people can trigger events through non-deliberate interactions such as being in a certain place at a certain time, the notion of interaction itself is fundamentally altered. The concept of technology use as a deliberate, conscious act becomes difficult to sustain and other models of interaction and communication will need to be developed. At the other extreme, digital technologies will continue to be used in more deliberate and engaged ways as media for self expression, community building, identity construction, self presentation and interpersonal relations. Understanding the complexity of the new forms of social relations and interactions will be required if we are to develop technology that can help us engage more effectively in these multiple worlds rather than stifle or reduce that engagement.

The new forms of engagement, then, require us to conceptualise users as embodied individuals who are part of a social, economic and political ecology, with desires, dreams, concerns and worries. The fact that we now live with technology and not just use it also means that people's forms of engagement with technology and the nature of their interactions with it are continuously changing and developing. At the same time, the distinction between designer and user will be harder to draw. Finally, understanding the new relationships between people and computers will involve asking questions about process, potential and change rather than attributes, capabilities and being.

Summary

HCI needs to move forward from concerns about the production and processing of information toward the design and evaluation of systems that enable human values to be achieved. Doing so requires HCI to shift its epistemological constraints away from their psychological roots towards other approaches, such as the philosophical, where conceptual sensitivity to meaning, purpose, and desire is possible. This suggests adding a fifth stage to HCI's conventional design/research model: a stage of conceptual analysis where we consider the human values we are trying to support or research. This affects the whole cycle of research and design, including how we understand the user, how we do studies in the field and the laboratory, how we reflect on the values sought in design, how we build prototypes and how we evaluate our designs. Finally, HCI researchers need a larger assembly of skills and know-how if they are to succeed, which has implications for the concepts, frameworks and theories of HCI.

4 Recommendations

Digital technologies have become a central feature of the 21st century and will become an even more fundamental and critical part of how we live. Our relationship with technology is changing and these changes raise fundamental questions about what we anticipate of computer systems in the future. What is clear is that digital technology in the world of 2020 will be as different from today as technology twenty five years ago was different from what we have now. These shifts and transformations in technology, and in our judgments about what we want computing to do, pose fundamental questions to those involved in Human-Computer Interaction. These questions require the HCI community to bring to the fore the fundamental human values shaping our everyday world and to use these to guide how HCI helps shape the ways people of all kinds will relate to computing technologies in 2020. This shift towards an emphasis on being human leads us to propose seven key recommendations to conclude this report.

We need to change HCI if it is to make sure ➔ that the future role of human computing is based on solid foundations.

Future Directions

We make seven recommendations for how to bring about a new way of undertaking HCI research and design and to make it more relevant to today's world. The goal is to find ways HCI can make a stronger impact on the relationship between people and technology at a personal, interpersonal and societal level.

Recommendation 1: Revisit research and design methods in HCI

As HCI has emerged as a distinct research area, the methods and techniques that have been used have altered over the years. Computer systems and the views of their users continue to change and diversify, so there is a need to be cognisant of the implications of these changes for the methods and techniques HCI will use in future. Thus, as we approach 2020, there is a need to:

- **Explore new ways of understanding users.** This will require the articulation of diverse methodologies. Over the last decade we have seen, for example, techniques rooted in design-based practices (such as cultural probes) come to prominence. These have complemented existing techniques of understanding that have emerged from scientific and engineering traditions – Human Factors and Cognitive Science, for instance. Other ways of extending and complementing existing techniques will be required beyond design; these may include views from more diverse disciplines and cultural traditions. The use of conceptual analysis as the first stage of a new HCI is a case in point. This technique derives from analytic philosophy, and entails clarifying the systems of meaning and value any particular set of activities involves.

- **Explore new ways of designing and making.** The design and building of prototypes of new devices will need to be undertaken in ways that are directed at particular kinds of user value. These will have to complement and extend existing ways of designing and building which emphasise usability and closeness of fit between prototyped and engineered solutions. In the future, more lightweight, rapid prototyping and design iteration processes will be required, and ones that will allow complex ecosystem experiences to be investigated as well as simpler, human-machine relationships. New prototyping tools and technologies will be especially important, allowing the rapid and easy assembly of novel hardware and software to test alongside and within everyday artefacts and living spaces.

- **Reconsider how to evaluate digital technologies.** There is a need to be sensitive to a shift away from the world of work, with its emphasis on productivity and efficiency, towards considerations of leisure and entertainment pursuits as well as towards aesthetic and cultural systems of value. Work will continue to be important, of course, but so too will these other domains and concerns. What will count as good in one domain may not apply in another; what is good for work may not be good for home life. The contrast here is not between, say, industry at work and idleness at home; it is between productivity and efficiency as one very limited set of explanatory criteria and a whole range of other criteria that are encompassed in the spectrum of human value. Evaluation tools, techniques and criteria must reflect this new richness and diversity.

Recommendation 2: Be explicit about the remit of HCI

Digital technology had a massive transformative effect on the 20th century. Most especially, it revolutionised the world of work. In the early part of the 21st century, we have started to see more widespread transformative effects raise a new set of issues of major societal, ethical and culture importance, examples of which were sketched out in Part 2 of this report. This raises the question of how far – or even whether – HCI, as a research area, should continue to extend itself. The dominant approach over the last twenty years has been to grow HCI by assimilating researchers and techniques from a broader and broader set of disciplines. As it has done so, the remit of HCI has grown. It is not longer clear that this approach is tenable. HCI cannot continue to broaden its concerns indefinitely. Should HCI be involved with any and all aspects of the interaction between people and digital technology? Clearly not. Should it concern itself with more than it has in the past? Clearly it should.

If we have asserted that HCI needs to encompass values rather than just performance, then this recommendation is that there is a need to specify what HCI specifically concerns itself with and what it does not encompass. It needs to say where its boundaries are so that it might offer substantive insight within them and recognise the need to draw on the expertise of other disciplines outside those boundaries.

As a case in point, one might suggest that HCI is concerned with the design of digital artefacts and landscapes. It creates new possibilities. Philosophy, meanwhile, is the discipline that explores and surveys the value landscape thus produced. Such explorations can lead HCI to develop new design possibilities, further altering and crafting that landscape. HCI undertakes one set of tasks; philosophy another. They are not merely steps in a process, however, but disciplines that, when properly understood for what they are, can be marshalled together.
.

Recommendation 3: Develop disciplinary techniques that allow HCI to collaborate with other research communities
The broadening and diversification of the digital in our everyday lives requires an increasingly broad set of disciplines with an interest in human values. These could

'In the future, more lightweight, rapid prototyping and design iteration processes will be required, ones that will allow complex ecosystem experiences to be investigated as well as simpler, human-machine relationships'

include architects, urban designers, economists and philosophers, to name but a few. Allied to the need to be aware of its boundaries, there is a need for HCI also to consider how to establish connections between itself and these other disciplines.

- **Disciplinary exchange** One requirement will be for HCI researchers to know how to converse with disciplines with very different traditions. Such sensitivities will need to be taught, as well as cultivated in practice. HCI researchers will need to know what other disciplines are good at and what those skills and techniques offer. For example, economists treat all activities – including value-laden ones – in terms of opportunity costs. For HCI, the ability to recognise where an opportunity cost analysis might be appropriate is clearly important, but the ability to carry out an analysis is not something that HCI researchers need to take on themselves. Economists are the experts in this and thus should be involved in such studies. Similarly, philosophers are very good at the investigation of ethics. Ethics will be clearly important in some domains HCI is seeking to design for. As with economists, HCI researchers need to understand what philosophers can do and why philosophy is important.

'Just as computing has gone beyond the interface, so, too, will HCI professionals need to move outside of the scientific community they have lived within and find ways to engage with society as a whole'

• **Beyond interdisciplinary boundaries** HCI should ask what might be the appropriate models for allowing interdisciplinary investigations to happen. There may be differences in how this can be achieved in academic research and in broader industrial practice where measures of contribution, success, and output may be different. Above all, the HCI community should be articulating good examples of interdisciplinary practice. This is an area where investment in basic research theories and approaches, in the elements of HCI competence and skill, and in the foundations of the philosophy of science are required.

Recommendation 4: Teach HCI to the young
This report has argued that the changing landscape being brought about by computers in our contemporary society has diverse and far-reaching implications for society. These implications are so complicated, rich and consequential that analysis of them should be introduced to people at an early age as a school topic. Teaching the practical skills of computing is one thing, and important in itself. But learning to use a word processor or spreadsheet tool will no longer be enough to understand the potential impact of computing in society. We suggest children should be introduced to the 'properties and possibilities

of computing' too. Only in this way can they develop sufficient understanding of computing to enable them to be fully computer-literate when they are adults, and help them to shape the world in relation to technology.

To achieve this will obviously require a change in the curricula of school teaching, most especially in ICT. But it will also require a shift in what parents expect their children to learn and reflect upon. Here the professional bodies of HCI, such as SIG CHI in North America and the BCS HCI Group in the UK, might help facilitate this change through helping to highlight the importance of HCI in public discourse about society in 2020.

Recommendation 5:
More advanced training for future HCI researchers
This report has argued for the need for HCI to be able to understand and design for an increasingly rich set of relationships between computer systems and users. However, we would suggest that, currently, there is a deficiency of HCI researchers with the breadth of training and experience to deliver on this broad canvas of concerns. It is imperative that HCI considers how it might scale-up its educational processes to develop a generation of researchers and practitioners that can comfortably engage with the broad set of disciplines we have outlined. In addition to increased support for training and the production of PhDs in this area, this will require HCI to revisit its curriculum. HCI students will need to be capable of using new, lightweight prototyping and coding tools (like 'phidgets'), for instance. They will also need greater methodological adroitness in choosing the right investigative techniques for the problems they are given, and they will need to be able to communicate to those outside of the discipline matters that might be of crucial importance to the other professions. Throughout their work, part of the training will be to explore ways to alert the public at large to the complex and value-laden design possibilities they are dealing

with. Just as computing has gone beyond the interface, so, too, will HCI professionals need to move outside of the scientific community they have lived within and find ways to engage with society as a whole.

Recommendation 6: Engage with government, policy and society

Throughout this report we have stressed the enormous impact that the relationship between people and technology will have in shaping all our futures. Given this, it seems to us certain that HCI will need to take increasingly seriously its role in these technologies. By the same token, it will also need to take seriously the societal importance of this role.

Consequently, HCI will need to engage actively in the construction of future government regulation and policy. So far this has been done in a limited way, for example in the area of the 'digital divide' or in an advisory role in issues to do with trust and security in computer systems. The emphasis has often been on technical issues or economics and not on the wider problems and possibilities of interaction. But we would argue that HCI should not confine itself to the problems of ensuring usability for the economically deprived, or in dealing with users with nefarious intentions. Rather, it should act in a wider advisory or steering role whenever there are salient consequences of the complex and diverse transformations that new forms of interaction with computers can achieve in all aspects of society.

Professional bodies will play a crucial role in alerting government to this new importance. They will also have a role in conveying considerations of values in HCI as of interest beyond the lab, indeed for everyone, at work and at home. Doing so will require HCI to build upon its considerable experience of engaging with users so as to

form stronger links with the general public. Above all, HCI needs to foster the public's concern with what computers might enable so that the society of 2020 is the one they seek and desire rather than the one they end up with.

Recommendation 7: Offer an inclusive future in 2020

This report has presented a vision of where we are heading by 2020 and the challenges this holds for HCI. It is all too easy to get excited by the future by thinking solely of the new capabilities and technologies and the advantages they will bring. However, there is also a need for some balance. There is a need for HCI, in particular, to recognise the global nature of future development. While radical technologies will continue to emerge, an equally exciting research agenda has to do with the use of computer systems in all parts of the world. It is imperative that HCI remembers that in 2020 the vast majority of those who rely on and use computer technologies might not have access to the most sophisticated and cutting-edge devices and applications. This will not mean, however, there will be those who have and those who do not have computing. It will mean, instead, that how computing is used and what computing is used for will be different depending on where we look. This diversity will reflect not simply economic realities but cultural differences. In other words, it will reflect differences in values.

In 1999, the science fiction writer William Gibson stated during a radio interview: 'As I've said many times, the future is already here. It's just not very evenly distributed.' One can read this as alluding to differences in economics. But we would prefer to read it differently. The last of the recommendations from this report is that, by 2020, HCI will need to be able to design for and support differences in human value, irrespective of the economic means of those seeking those values. In this way, the future can be different and diverse because people want it to be.

Appendix: What is Human-Computer Interaction?

Human-Computer Interaction (HCI) is a term used to refer to the understanding and designing of different relationships between people and computers. At the outset, in the late 1970s, the main concern of HCI was 'usability'. Since then, HCI has established an impressive track record for developing and applying all manner of design and evaluation methods to ensure that technologies are easy to learn and easy to use. So, for example, it has produced a large body of insightful data or evidence on what is 'good' and 'bad' usability, developed methods for the production and analysis of such evidence, and developed an armoury of tried and tested techniques that HCI practitioners can depend upon in daily practice to ensure usability.

More recently, HCI has begun to develop techniques for inventing things that are not just usable but useful. It has also begun to investigate the relationships between people that computers and computer networks enable, such as patterns of behaviour between people and within social groups.

It is hardly surprising that nearly all computer and communications companies, as well as companies developing Web applications or computer games, have HCI practitioners either scattered throughout their product development groups, or as centralised resources, or even both. Nearly every company of any stature in the technology industry has experts in HCI. As computing technology has begun to pervade a wider spectrum of products, including vehicles and white goods (such as ovens and fridges for instance), so other companies are beginning to employ HCI professionals too. And within organisations, HCI expertise is of increasing importance as efforts are made to improve the efficiency of their intranets, a concept which covers such things as internal documentation, information sharing and administrative

functions. The result of these developments is that HCI has become an integral part of the design process across the board, although it can still be the case that other demands in design and development get prioritised, meaning that the impact of HCI comes 'too little, too late'.

Irrespective of its success or failure in particular instances, the importance of HCI is such that knowledge about it (if not about the nuances of its techniques) has seeped into the consciousness of nearly all members of our society. Terms such as 'usability', 'user-friendliness', 'human factors' and 'user experience' signal the impact of HCI in such diverse outlets as advice columns, guides to consumers, cartoons and even advertising. Consumers of all kinds increasingly see usability – as one of the dimensions that HCI has expertise in – as a way to choose from a vast array of similar technological products.

The evolution of HCI

Central to the practice of HCI is a set of concepts, techniques and methods that underpin research, and help practitioners make decisions when designing interaction with technology. These have evolved over the past 30 years.

The earliest techniques and concepts of HCI, many of which were first formed in the late 1970s, had their roots in an amalgam of thinking that emphasised the tradition of Human Factors Engineering. This approach saw the primary metaphor for human-computer interaction as being one of 'human-machine coupling'; as one that entailed optimising the 'fit' between the user and machine. Key elements of HCI still stem from this influence and associated metaphors and models.

For example, a characteristic and successful methodology for predicting and analysing user behaviour – the idea that a user needs to fit the computer – is through the application of Fitt's Law (1954). This is a model of human movement which is used by researchers to predict, for example, the time required for a user to click on a given sized target using a mouse. It has been used widely as a method for evaluating systems where the time to physically locate an object is critical to the task in hand or where there is limited space on the device for the placement of digital objects in an interface. For instance, a number of mobile phone companies used it to predict text entry rates for different input methods using a 12-key cell phone keypad. It can also be used to determine the size and location of so-called soft keys on smart phones that only have a touch-sensitive screen and no real buttons.

As HCI has developed, so there has been a turn towards a greater emphasis on aspects of the mind and less on the behaviour of the body; less on pointing and clicking with fingers and more with how people understand and come to recognise objects and processes. There was a 'cognitive revolution' at the heart of much of HCI research in the 1980s and 1990s that reflected this shift. This was presented most famously by the Xerox PARC researchers Card, Moran and Newell in their book, *The Psychology of Human-Computer Interaction* (1984). In this view, the human is seen as an information processor, with inputs (mainly visual), mental processing, and outputs (keyboard strokes, mouse actions and so on), which then in turn 'input' information or data into the computer.

This approach enabled the production of generalisable models of human interaction, somewhat akin to the models produced by the earlier Human Factors approach. One notable method was the Goals, Operators, Methods and Selection Rules (or 'GOMS') model, which allowed researchers to develop a model of a user undertaking a particular cognitive task. This allowed them to optimise

technology for a particular activity. In one famous study (Gray et al, 1995), the technique was used to evaluate a novel workstation proposed for telephone company operators, demonstrating that the operators' performance on new workstations would, in fact, be slower than the existing workstations.

This new more cognitive approach built on rather than displaced the prior Human Factors-oriented HCI. The combination produced considerable dividends. Indeed, many would argue that much of what we now take for granted – including advances in the Graphical User Interface, the speed with which 'points and clicks' can be made, and more – are the consequence of this accumulation of cognitive and Human Factors approaches.

During the 1990s, the concerns of HCI started to shift towards communication between people enabled by computers. This mirrored the growth in communication networks linking computers together. If, before, the concern of HCI had been to determine how to let users efficiently and effectively interact with a computer, now researchers started asking how users might interact with each other via a computer. Researchers with a background in more socially-oriented sciences, like Anthropology and Sociology, began to engage with HCI. These disciplines not only emphasised the effects of computing on groups of people (or users) but also how computers were interpreted and appropriated by those same groups of users. These disciplines also brought a concern for the social, emotional, as well as technical ways in which the relationship with technology develops. Eventually the approaches of these disciplines were amalgamated so that concerns that had been central before, such as those related to cognitive processing and so forth, were supplemented (and in some ways replaced) by more complex social modelling views and techniques.

At the same time, there was a growing realisation that design, as a set of related practices in its own right, should also become an important part of HCI. If it was the case that part of the goal of HCI was to 'design' beyond interaction between user and machine and beyond even computer-mediated interaction between people, then other concerns might be relevant too, such as cultural and aesthetic desires. Science and social science perspectives were thought too limited to capture the essence of what this meant. And so it was that by the mid-1990s designers and 'design practice' became heavily involved in HCI. Notions of 'interaction design' came to the fore. These emphasised practice-based approaches to the exploration of the relationship between computers and people and placed less stress on the modelling of the user, as had been the case before.

At the start of the 21st century, HCI is an interdisciplinary field which has undergone enormous change. In terms of a science or a discipline, these changes have occurred over a very short time. HCI now encompasses many philosophies, perspectives and types of expertise. There are multiple and overlapping groups of researchers, some emphasising design, others evaluation, and yet others user modelling. These experts all work within a complex space, each examining different aspects of human-computer interaction. Different techniques are used, depending on different goals. If the goal is to incrementally improve a routine task – shave seconds from the time to enter each of millions of census forms, for example – then a carefully controlled large-scale experiment with rigorous statistical analysis is essential. If the goal is to find glaring problems in the initial version of a new consumer application, a relatively quick iterative design evaluation may be better. Understanding a complex social task may require a long-term field investigation to understand the setting where the technology may be placed. To identify an engaging

design, rapid generation and exploration of alternatives may be best, and so on.

This diversity is reflected in numerous textbooks concerning HCI *(see Bibliography)* as well as websites and journals (*Human-Computer Interaction*, *International Journal of Human-Computer Studies* – and magazines such as *Interactions* and *User Experience Magazine*). As HCI has developed, so has the number of international conferences devoted to it, with over 20 or so conferences per year at the current time. And of course this book has its origins in just such a conference. A good overview of an increasingly diverse field is provided online by the HCI Bibliography – http://www.hcibib.org/ – which provides a useful starting point for interested readers. Further suggestions are also presented in the Bibliography.

Bibliography

General books about HCI

There are a great many books and reference materials for HCI. Here is a selected list of books and articles, including classic and new texts that will give the lay reader a good introduction to the discipline:

Baecker, R, Grudin, J, Buxton, W, Greenberg, S (eds) (1995) *Readings in Human-Computer Interaction: Toward the Year 2000*. 2nd ed. San Francisco: Morgan Kaufmann.

Buxton, B (2007) *Sketching User Experience: Getting the Design Right and the Right Design*. San Francisco: Morgan Kaufmann.

Carroll, JM (ed) (2002) *Human-Computer Interaction in the New Millennium*. New York: ACM Press.

Dix, A, Finlay, J, Abowd, G and Beale, R (2003) *Human-Computer Interaction*. 3rd ed. Prentice Hall.

Jacko, J and Sears, A (2007) *Human-Computer Interaction Handbook. 2nd ed.* Mahwah, New Jersey: Lawrence Erlbaum.

Jones, J and Marsden G (2005) *Mobile Interaction Design*. London: Wiley & Sons.

McCarthy, J and Wright, P (2004) *Technology as Experience*. Boston: MIT Press.

Norman, D (2007) *The Design of Future Things*. New York: Basic Books.

Norman, D (1988) *The Psychology of Everyday Things*. New York: Basic Books.

Raskin, J, (2000) *The Humane Interface: New directions for designing interactive systems*. Boston: Addison-Wesley.

Rogers, Y, Sharp, H, and Preece, J (2007) *Interaction Design: Beyond Human Computer Interaction*. 2nd ed. Hoboken, New Jersey: Wiley.

Rosson, M and Carroll, J (2001) *Usability Engineering: Scenario-Based Development of Human-Computer Interaction*. New York: Morgan Kaufmann.

Shneiderman, B (2002) *Leonardo's Laptop*. Boston: MIT Press.

Thimbleby, H (2007) *Press On: Principles of interaction programming*. Boston: MIT Press.

Thomas, JC (1995) 'Usability Engineering in 2020' in Nielsen, J (ed), *Advances in human-computer interaction*. Norwood, New Jersey: Ablex (Intellect).

Websites
Good sources of websites, blogs, videos, software etc on interaction design and HCI can be found at these two websites:
http://www.id-book.com/starters.htm
http://www.hcibib.org/

Other relevant or influential books and articles:

Anderson, C (2007) *The Long Tail: How Endless Choice is Creating Unlimited Demand*. London: Random House.

Clark, A (2004) *Natural-born Cyborgs: Minds, Technologies, and the Future of Human Intelligence*. New York: Oxford University Press.

Cousins, N (1966) 'The Computer and the Poet', *Saturday Review*, July 23rd.

Dourish, P (2004) *Where the Action Is: The Foundations of Embodied Interaction*. Boston: MIT Press.

Emmott, S. J., Shapiro, E., Rison, S., Phillips, A., and Herbert, A. J (2006) *Towards 2020 Science*.UK: Microsoft Research Ltd.

Greenfield, A (2006) *Everyware: The Dawning Age of Ubiquitous Computing*. New York: New Preachpit Press.

Jenson, S (2002) *The Simplicity Shift: Innovative Design Tactics in a Corporate World*. Cambridge, UK: Cambridge University Press.

Rheingold, H (2002) *Smart Mobs: The Next Social Revolution*. Cambridge, Mass: Perseus.

Rogers, Y (2006) 'Moving on from Weiser's vision of calm computing: Engaging UbiComp experiences', in Dourish, P and Friday, A (eds) *Ubicomp 2006 Proceedings*, LNCS 4206, pp 404-421. Berlin: Springer-Verlag.

Sellen, A and Harper, R (2001) *The Myth of the Paperless Office*. Boston: MIT Press.

Weiser, M (1991) 'The Computer for the Twenty-First Century' in *Scientific American*, pp 94-10, September.

Reflections on the History of HCI

The following books and articles provide more background reading to accompany the Appendix on the history of HCI, including the specific references in that section:

Card, S, Moran, T and Newell, A (1984) *The Psychology of Human-Computer Interaction*. Hillsdale, New Jersey: Lawrence Erlbaum.

Erickson, T and McDonald, DW (2008) *HCI Remixed. Reflections on Works That Have Influenced the HCI Community*. Boston: MIT Press.

Fitts, P (1954) 'The information capacity of the human motor system in controlling amplitude of movement' in *Journal of Experimental Psychology*, 47, 381-391.

Gray, WD, John, BE, Stuart, R, Lawrence, D and Atwood, ME (1995) 'GOMS meets the phone company: Analytic modeling applied to real world problems,' in Baecker, R, Grudin, J, Buxton, W and Greenberg, S (eds) *Readings in Human Computer Interaction: Towards the Year 2000*, pp 634-639, San Francisco: Morgan-Kaufmann.

Grudin, J (2007) 'A Moving Target: The Evolution of Human-Computer Interaction', in Sears, A and Jacko, J (eds), *Human-Computer Interaction Handbook: Fundamentals, Evolving Technologies and Emerging Applications*, pp1-24, Mahwah, New Jersey: Lawrence Erlbaum Associates.

Harrison, S, Tatar, D, Sengers, P (2007) 'The Three Paradigms of HCI,' *alt.chi, CHI' 07*. New York: ACM Press.

References from the Case Studies in Part 3

These papers describe the original research referred to in the case studies in Part 3:

Brown, B, Taylor, A, Izadi, S, Sellen, A and Kaye, J (2007) 'Locating Family Values: A Field Trial of the Whereabouts Clock', in *Proceedings of UbiComp 2007*. Godalming: Springer Verlag.

Taylor, A, Harper, R, Swan, L, Izadi, S, Sellen, A, and Perry, M (2007) 'Homes that make us smart,' in *Personal and Ubiquitous Computing* (special issue "At Home with IT: Pervasive Computing in the Domestic Space"), Number 5, June 2007

Harper, R, Randall, D, Smyth, N, Evans, C, Heledd, L and Moore, R (2008) 'The past is a different place: They do things differently there' in *Designing Interactive Systems 2008 (DIS)*, New York: ACM Press. pp 271-280.

Harper, R, Randall, D, Smyth, N, Evans, C, Heledd, L and Moore, R (2007) 'Thanks for the memory' in *Interact: HCI 2007*, Lancaster: British Computer Society, September, pp39-43, Vol 2.

Harper, R, Regan, T, Al Mosawi, K, Rubens, S and Rouncefield, M (2007) 'Trafficking: design for the viral exchange of multimedia content', *Mobile HCI 2007*. Singapore: ACM, Research Publishing, pp49-64.

Sellen, A, Fogg, A, Hodges, S, Rother, C and Wood, K (2007) 'Do life-logging technologies support memory for the past? An experimental study using SenseCam.' *Proceedings of CHI '07*, available online at: http://portal.acm.org.

HCI 2020 Forum Participants

Christopher Bishop

Chris Bishop, Deputy Director of Microsoft Research, Cambridge UK, has a Chair in Computer Science at the University of Edinburgh, and is a Fellow of Darwin College Cambridge. He has been elected a Fellow of the Royal Academy of Engineering. Research interests include probabilistic approaches to machine-learning, as well as their application to fields such as computer vision.

Gilbert Cockton

Gilbert Cockton is Research Chair in HCI at the University of Sunderland in the north east of England. He is a Fellow of both the Royal Society for the Arts and the British Computer Society, and has published extensively on usability and accessibility, grounded- and worth/value-centred design, as well as notations and architectures for interactive software.

Barry Brown

Barry Brown is currently an Associate Professor of Communications at UC San Diego and Equator Research Fellow, Glasgow University. His recent work has focused on the sociology and design of leisure technologies. Recent publications include studies of activities as diverse as games, tourism, museum visiting, the use of maps, television watching and sport spectating.

Thomas Erickson

Thomas Erickson is an interaction designer and researcher at the IBM TJ Watson Research Center in New York, to which he telecommutes from his home in Minneapolis. His primary interest is in studying and designing systems that enable groups of all sizes to interact coherently and productively over networks.

AJ Brush

AJ Brush works at Microsoft Research as a researcher in the VIBE group. Her main research interest is human-computer interaction with a focus on computer-supported cooperative work. She enjoys investigating how technology can help people and groups with everyday problems.

David Frohlich

David Frohlich is Director of Digital World Research Centre at the University of Surrey and Professor of Interaction Design. He joined the Centre in January 2005 to establish a new research agenda on user-centred innovation for the consumer market.

Matthew Chalmers

Matthew Chalmers is a Reader at the University of Glasgow. He combines ubicomp theory, infrastructure and interaction, explored via systems for tourism, health and leisure. He has published widely on topics including mobile multiplayer games, the use of philosophical hermeneutics to design computer systems, and the nature of the museum visit experience.

Bill Gaver

Bill Gaver is a professor at Goldsmiths College in London. Bill has pursued research on interactive technologies for over 20 years, following a trajectory that led from experimental science to design. Currently he focuses on design-led methodologies and innovative products for everyday life.

Adam Greenfield

Adam Greenfield is a writer, consultant and instructor at New York University's Interactive Telecommunications Program. His first book, *Everyware: The dawning age of ubiquitous computing*, has been acclaimed as 'the first work on the topic suitable for general audiences'. He lives and works in New York City with his wife, artist Nurri Kim.

Lars Erik Holmquist

Lars Erik Holmquist is an Associate Professor and leads the Future Applications Lab at the Mobile Life Center in Kista, Sweden, where his employment is shared between the Swedish Institute of Computer Science and the University of Stockholm.

Jonathan Grudin

Jonathan Grudin is a Principal Researcher at Microsoft Research, where he has been since 1998. Immediately prior to Microsoft he was Professor of Information and Computer Science at the University of California, Irvine. He has also taught at Aarhus University, Keio University, and the University of Oslo.

Kristina Höök

Professor Kristina Höök is a full professor at Department of Computer and Systems Science, Stockholm University/KTH since February 2003. She is also a laboratory manager of the interaction lab at SICS. The focus of her group is on social and affective interaction, and narrative intelligence, often in mobile settings.

Richard Harper

Richard Harper is Senior Researcher at Microsoft Research in Cambridge, UK and Professor of Socio-Digital Systems at the University of Surrey. His most recent book is *Fieldwork and Design* (with Dave Randall and Mark Rouncefield, Kluwer, 2007). He is currently completing a new book called *Texture: Communication in the 21st Century* (MIT Press), due out summer 2008.

Steve Howard

Steve Howard is the Head of Information Systems at the University of Melbourne. Steve left school at 16 and for four years worked in an engineering factory. He then meandered through an education in psychology, ergonomics and HCI, and the interaction between technology and people has remained his interest. He focuses on the application of IT to areas of real social need.

Andrew Herbert

Andrew Herbert is a distinguished engineer and managing director of Microsoft Research in Cambridge, England. Initially joining Microsoft Research in 2001 as an assistant director, he succeeded the founding director, Roger Needham, in March 2003.

Shahram Izadi

Shahram Izadi is a researcher at Microsoft Research in Cambridge, UK. His research centres on interactive surfaces, specifically looking at a future where diverse display technologies are cheap and all around us. He is interested in exploring interaction techniques beyond the keyboard and mouse, utilising hands, tangible objects and haptic feedback.

Scott Jenson

Scott Jenson is an interface designer at Google. He has been doing user interface design and strategic planning for 20 years. He worked at Apple until 1993 on System 7, Newton, and the Apple Human Interface Guidelines. For three years he was the director of Symbian's DesignLab, managing 20 people to design, prototype, user-test, and specify future mobile products.

Matt Jones

Matt Jones is a Reader in Computer Science, helping to set up the Future Interaction Technology Lab at Swansea University. He has worked on mobile interaction issues for the past twelve years and has published a large number of articles in this area.

Sergi Jordà

Sergi Jordà is an Associate Professor in the Technology Department of the Pompeu Fabra University in Barcelona. Since then he has taught courses as diverse as OOP, HCI, Computer Music and Interactive Digital Arts. He is best known as the inventor of the Reactable, a tabletop new musical instrument hand-picked by Icelandic songstress Björk for her 2007 world tour.

Rui José

Rui José was born in Portugal, where he did his undergraduate and MSc studies in Computing at the University of Minho. In 2001, he received his PhD degree in Computer Science (Distributed Systems) from Lancaster University, UK. He is now an Assistant Professor at the Information Systems Department of the University of Minho.

Jofish Kaye

Jofish Kaye is a doctoral candidate in Information Science at Cornell University. His dissertation research is concerned with producing theory and methodology for the evaluation of experience-focused – as opposed to task-focused – HCI.

Wendy Kellogg

Wendy Kellogg manages Social Computing at IBM's TJ Watson Research Center. Her current work focuses on computer-mediated communication (CMC), including social translucence and virtual worlds. She holds a PhD in Cognitive Psychology from the University of Oregon and writes in the fields of HCI and CSCW. Wendy chaired CHI 2005 Papers and the CHI '94 conference.

Boriana Koleva

Boriana Koleva is a lecturer in the School of Computer Science at the University of Nottingham. Her research area is the field of Human-Computer Interaction, with a particular emphasis on Ubicomp interfaces. Her thesis work focused on mixed reality boundaries which link virtual and physical spaces.

Steven Kyffin

Steven Kyffin (Master of Design, Industrial Design, Royal College of Art, London) is Senior Director of Philips' Design Research & Innovation programmes. In this function he directs the Ideas (Innovation) Engine of Philips Design and the programme of Design Research in Philips Electronics worldwide.

Paul Luff

Paul Luff is a Reader at Kings College, London. His research involves the study of everyday work and interaction drawing upon detailed analysis of audio-visual recordings of human conduct. These analyses are frequently utilised within projects that seek to develop innovative kinds of technologies such as enhanced media spaces, robots and augmented paper.

Jun Rekimoto

Jun Rekimoto is a professor at the University of Tokyo and director of the Interaction Lab, Sony Computer Science Laboratories. He received the BSc, the MSc and the PhD in Information Science from Tokyo Institute of Technology in 1984, 1986, and 1996, respectively. He was appointed to the SIGCHI Academy in 2007.

Gary Marsden

Gary Marsden is an Associate Professor in the Department of Computer Science at the University of Cape Town in South Africa, where he has worked since 1999. Originally he worked in the field of Mobile Interaction Design, but since moving to Africa, his research has focused more on the use of ICT for human development.

Tom Rodden

Tom Rodden is Professor of Interactive Systems at the Mixed Reality Laboratory (MRL) at the University of Nottingham, where he directed the Equator IRC and is now an EPSRC Senior Research Fellow. His research focuses on the development of new technologies to support users within the real world and new forms of interactive technology that mix physical and digital interaction.

Tom Moher

Tom Moher is Associate Professor of Computer Science at the University of Illinois at Chicago (UIC). He also holds an adjunct Associate Professor position in the College of Education there, and serves on the steering committee for the UIC Learning Sciences programme.

Yvonne Rogers

Yvonne Rogers is a professor of HCI at the Open University, and a visiting professor at Indiana University. She researches and teaches in the areas of HCI, Ubiquitous computing and CSCW. A particular focus is augmenting and extending everyday learning and work activities with novel technologies including mobile, wireless, handheld and pervasive computing.

Kenton O'Hara

Kenton O'Hara is a Senior Research Scientist at HP Labs Bristol in the Mobile and Media Systems Lab. His research explores the social and behavioural factors that shape the design and use of emerging technologies.

Mark Rouncefield

Mark Rouncefield is an ethnographer and sociologist and is a Senior Research Fellow in the Department of Computing. He is also a Microsoft European Research Fellow studying social interaction and mundane technologies.

Abigail Sellen

Abigail Sellen is a Senior Researcher in Microsoft's Cambridge UK Lab and co-manager of the Socio-Digital Systems group, an interdisciplinary group with a focus on the human perspective in computing. She has published widely in HCI, but her current pre-occupation is with designing technologies for the home and to support human memory.

Wes Sharrock

Wes Sharrock is Professor of Sociology at the University of Manchester, UK. He has had a career-long interest in the philosophy of social science, especially the implications of Wittgenstein's philosophy for social science, including the philosophy of mind, involving an opposition to reductionism in all its forms. He also has a long-standing interest in observational studies of work.

Alex Taylor

Alex Taylor is a member of the Socio-Digital Systems Group at Microsoft Research, Cambridge, UK. He has undertaken investigations into the mundane aspects of everyday life. For example, examining paper lists, fridge doors, junk drawers and pottering. Through these investigations he has developed an unhealthy preoccupation with hoarding, dirt and clutter.

John Thomas

John Thomas is a researcher at IBM. Prior to IBM, John managed research on the psychology of aging at Harvard Medical School and led the AI Lab at NYNEX Science and Technology. His interests have spanned natural language processing, audio systems, and speech synthesis. More recently he has worked on the business uses of storytelling, pattern languages and e-learning.

Michael Twidale

Michael Twidale is an Associate Professor of the Graduate School of Library and Information Science, University of Illinois. His research interests include computer supported cooperative work, collaborative information retrieval, user interface design, museum informatics, ubiquitous learning, in interaction of learning work and play, and rapid prototyping and evaluation techniques.

Alessandro Valli

Alessandro is an Italian interactive systems engineer and experience designer at iO. He received his MSc and PhD degrees in computer engineering from the University of Florence, in 2000 and in 2004. In 2001 he started focusing on the topic of natural interaction between humans and machines.

Geoff Walsham

Geoff Walsham is a Professor of Management Studies (Information Systems) at the Judge Business School, University of Cambridge, UK. In addition to Cambridge, he has held academic posts at the University of Lancaster in the UK where he was Professor of Information Management, the University of Nairobi in Kenya, and Mindanao State University in the Philippines.

Steve Whittaker

Steve Whittaker is Chair in Information Studies at Sheffield University. His research interests are in the theory, design and evaluation of collaborative systems, as well as multimedia access and retrieval. In the past he has designed and built many novel interactive systems.

Ken Wood

Ken Wood is Deputy Director of Microsoft's Cambridge UK Research Lab, with responsibility for the lab's business-facing activities, including technology transfer, incubation, licensing, spin-offs, and other models for exploiting the intellectual property generated by the research groups. Ken also heads the Computer-Mediated Living research group.

Jian Wang

Jian Wang is a principal researcher and Assistant Managing Director at Microsoft Research Asia. He manages the machine-learning group, the data-centric computing group and Microsoft's adCenter adLab in Beijing. Dr Wang's research interests are ink and pen computing, large-scale data and information processing, seamless computing, and human cognition.

Adrian Woolard

Adrian Woolard leads collaborative research projects within the Research & Innovation Group, BBC Future Media & Technology. The Innovation team is a small multi-disciplinary unit focused on exploring the changing relationships between media, audience and technology in the emerging multi-genre, multi-platform environment.

Peter Wright

Peter Wright is research Professor of Human-Centred Design in the Art and Design Research Centre (ADRC), Sheffield Hallam University, Sheffield, UK. He joined ADRC in October 2006. Prior to this he was Reader in Human-Computer Interaction in the Department of Computer Science at the University of York, UK.

Oren Zuckerman

Oren Zuckerman is a faculty member at the Interdisciplinary Center (IDC), Herzliya, Israel. Oren teaches and researches innovative forms of human-computer interaction, with special focus on physical interaction and cross-platform media experiences. Oren earned his Master's and PhD degrees at MIT's Media Laboratory.

Glossary

Actuators

Typically very small electro-mechanical devices that create or inhibit movement of one kind or another. Vibrators on mobile phones are an example of actuators.

Bayes' theorem

A mathematical relationship between probabilities which allows the probabilities to be updated in light of new information. It can be used to provide a formal foundation for Machine-Learning (see below).

BlueTooth

BlueTooth provides a way exchange information between devices such as mobiles, PCs, digital cameras, and video game consoles over a secure, globally unlicensed short-range radio frequency.

Brain-computer interaction

The use of brain signal monitoring to convey action commands to a computer.

Camera input

The use of visual signals, from a camera, to provide instructions for a computer.

Conceptual analysis

A philosophical technique that entails the investigation of the relationships between ideas and in particular, their linguistic formula. This book proposes it as a new first stage of HCI's design/research model.

Digital footprint

The name given to the auditable traces of an individual's interaction with computers.

E-paper

A display technology designed to mimic the appearance of ordinary ink on paper. Unlike a conventional display, which uses a backlight to illuminate its pixels, e-paper reflects light like ordinary paper and is capable of holding text and images indefinitely without drawing electricity. E-paper often uses a plastic substrate and electronics, so that the display is bendable.

Ethnography

The term used to describe studies of people in everyday contexts, usually contrasted with studies of user behaviour in laboratory settings.

Graphical user interface (GUI)

The use of graphical icons (such as folders and windows) for the objects one can interact with on a computer screen, usually by pointing and clicking on them with a mouse.

Flexible displays

Screen technologies that are bendable: such as e-paper.

Indirect interaction

The use of an object to control an object other than itself (such as a mouse to control a pointer on the computer screen).

Intelligent systems

Computer systems that mimic some aspects of human intelligence, such as the ability to perceive and act on the environment, to make complex decisions, to learn, and to make inferences about a human's intentions.

Machine-learning

A statistical technique that allows a computer to 'learn' how to perform a task by analysing a set of 'training data' which represents examples of the task and the required solution. It has widespread applications including handwriting recognition, computer vision, robotics, bioinformatics and data mining. This technique is often based on Bayes' theorem (see above).

Mash-ups

When users bring applications together in novel ways, such as when they combine a database of music sound tracks with a video editor to create new audio-visual experiences.

MEMS

Short for 'micro-electromechanical systems', MEMS is a micro fabrication technology that embeds mechanical devices, such as fluid sensors, mirrors, actuators, vibration sensors and valves, in semiconductor chips.

Multi-touch

Systems which support interaction using more than one finger at a time, and more than one hand. Such sensing devices are inherently also able to accommodate multiple users which is especially useful for interaction surfaces such as digital tabletops.

Natural interaction

Typically used to refer to interaction techniques for the computer which are modelled on the ways people interact with physical objects in the everyday world. Using two hands to manipulate digital photos on an interactive tabletop is one example.

Neural networks

The modern usage of the term refers to artificial neural networks, a way of building computer models inspired by the ways in which biological neural networks are structured and process information.

OLED

'Organic light emitting diode' – elements whose emissive electroluminescent layer is composed of a film of organic compounds. These can be used for displays and need no backlight, hence can be thinner, lighter and use less power than conventional displays.

Phidgets

Small, simple, electro-mechanical and software-controlled devices that can be easily assembled together and programmed for prototyping purposes. These arose from a research project led by Saul Greenberg at the University of Calgary.

Podcasting

A podcast is a collection of digital media files distributed over the Internet using syndication feeds for playback on portable media players and PCs. The term, like 'radio', can refer either to the content itself or to the method by which it is syndicated.

Pressure input

The use of different levels of pressure on a screen or other computer device to create different kinds of input to a computer.

Recognition algorithms

Computer code or algorithms designed to instruct the computer on how to identify and distinguish between various kinds of objects, either in the physical world (such as faces) or in the digital world (such as letters scribbled on a tablet computer).

RSI

A repetitive strain injury (RSI) is any of a loose group of conditions resulting from overuse of a tool, such as a computer and more particularly a computer keyboard and mouse, that requires repeated movements.

RFID

Radio-frequency identification: an automatic identification method, relying on storing and remotely retrieving data using devices called RFID tags. An RFID tag is an object that can be applied to or incorporated into a product, animal, or person for the purpose of identification using radio waves.

RSS feeds

RSS (formally 'RDF site summary', known colloquially as 'really simple syndication') is a family of Web feed formats used to publish frequently updated content such as blog entries, news headlines or podcasts. RSS feeds can contain either a summary of content from an associated website or the full text.

Sensed interaction

The use of sensors, such as for light, movement and sound, to create a signal for the computer to process.

Skype (Skyping)

Skype is a proprietary Internet telephony (VoIP) network that allows registered users to make telephone calls over the internet.

Smart fabrics

The embedding of sensors and other electronics in textiles such they change a property of themselves to reflect a computational command, eg Italian firm Luminex's idea of weaving fibre-optics into fabric, so the wearer can light up a room when they enter it.

97

SMS-texting

Short Message Service (SMS) is a communications protocol allowing the interchange of short text messages (of up to 160 characters) between mobile telephone devices. Texting is used as a colloquial synonym for the use of SMS.

Social metadata

Labels and other high-level descriptors of digital data created by multiple users. Factoring in the opinions, naming conventions, web habits, locations, and behaviours of 'ordinary' people and their friends could 'humanise' machine algorithms, and lead to hundreds of fascinating applications.

Tangible interface

An interface that uses the manipulation of physical objects to create instructions for the computer. This can mean either using physical objects in conjunction with computers, or embedding computers within the objects themselves.

UGC

'User-generated content': the kind of material produced by users and made available for broadcast on social network sites like YouTube and Flickr. UGC is normally contrasted with editorialised content, content subject to some kind of professional production.

Vibro-tactile display

A technique that uses vibration as the output from computers to create new kinds of sensory experiences for users.

Web 2.0

The name for web-usage and tools that emphasise user-created content and experiences, and in particular the user-creation of novel amalgams of applications.

WiFi

A wireless technology brand owned by the WiFi Alliance intended to improve the interoperability of wireless local area network products based on the IEEE 802.11 standards. Common applications include Internet and voice over internet protocol, such as Skype, phone access, gaming, and network connectivity for consumer electronics.

Picture Credits

The authors express their gratitude to the individuals and companies below for generously supplying the images for this report.

Page 13: The world of the future – Philips Design

Page 14-15: Four Computer Eras Diagram – Nick Duffield

Page 16: The Reactable – Universitat Pompeu Fabra, Barcelona

Page 17: The HotHand – Source Audio LLC, Massachusetts

Page 18: Animated Textiles – Studio subTela at the Hexagram Institute, Montreal, Canada

Page 20: The iCAT robot hardware platform – Philips Design

Page 21: The Rovio robotic webcam – WowWee Robotics

Page 22: Gordon Bell – Mark Richards, IEEE Spectrum

Page 24: Twitter Blocks – Twitter Inc, San Francisco

Page 25: The Ambient Periscope – Equator Project, University of Sussex

Page 26: The Ambient Wood – Equator Project, University of Sussex

Page 27: Audiovox's Digital Message Center – Audiovox

Page 28: Sony's EyeToy – Sony Computer Entertainment

Page 29: A man in Cape Town, South Africa, selling mobile phones – Gary Marsden, University of Cape Town

Page 30: Visa Micro Tag – Visa

Page 33: Tokyo artistic installation, 'Duality' – Design agency, ART+COM

Page 36: Electronic Sensing Jewelry – Philips Design

Page 38: The History Tablecloth – Interaction Research Studio (Goldsmiths College, University of London)

Page 40: I-Garment – I-Garment consortium (YDreams, designer Miguel Rios and the Instituto de Telecomunicações, Lisbon)

Page 48: Vodafone's young musicians – Vodafone

Page 53: The Kiss Communicator – IDEO, Palo Alt

Page 62: Phidgets – Saul Greenberg, University of Calgary